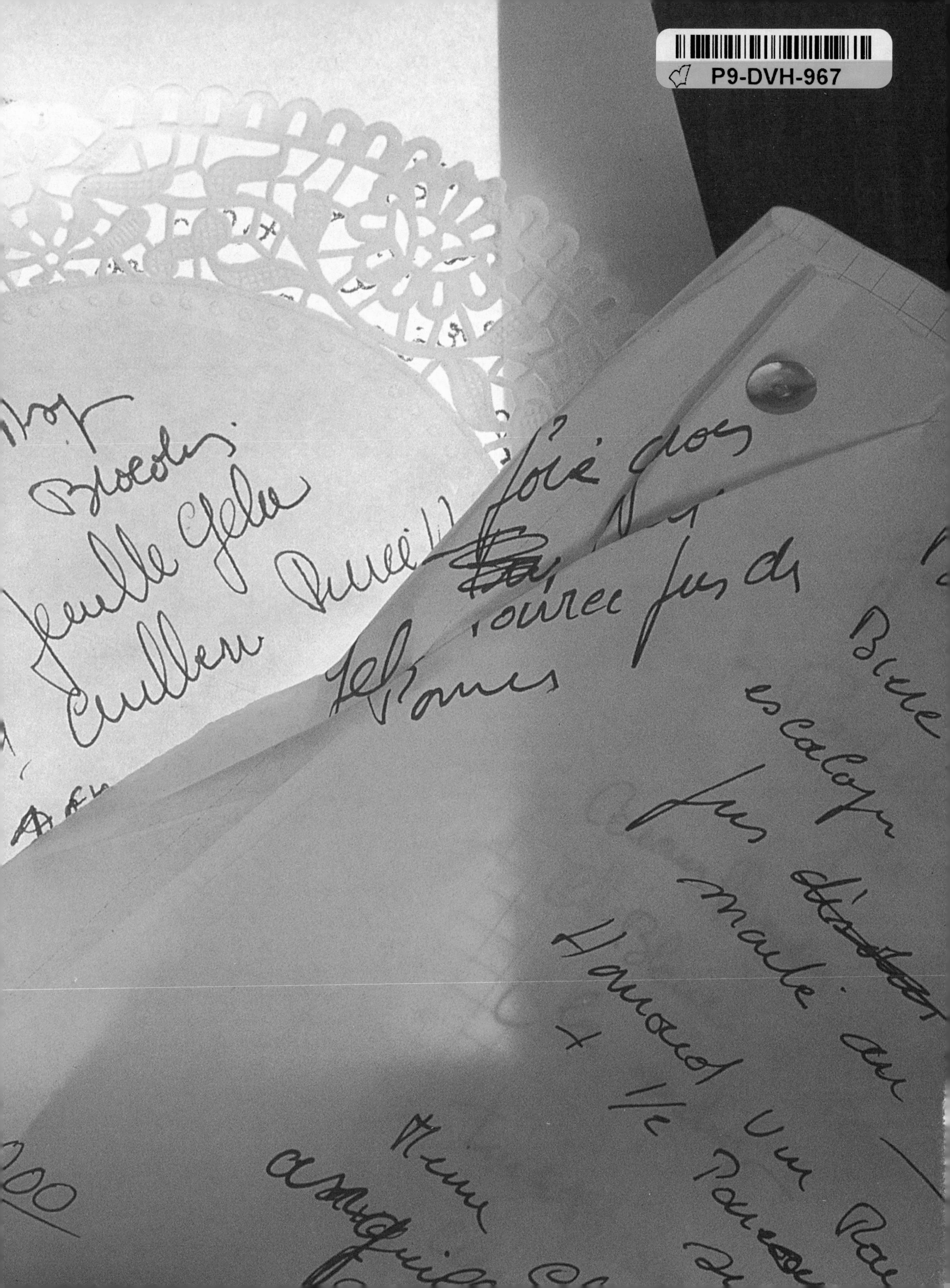

# New Entertaining
## in the French Style

*To Denise, my wife, and my daughter, Cordélia, who make every meal a celebration.*

Copyright © 1996 Flammarion, Paris

Published in 1997 and distributed in the U.S. by
Stewart, Tabori & Chang,
a division of U.S. Media Holdings, Inc.
115 West 18th Street, New York, NY 10011

Distributed in Canada by General Publishing Co. Ltd.
30 Lesmill Road, Don Mills, Ontario, Canada M3B 2T6
Distributed in Australia by Peribo Pty Ltd.
58 Beaumont Road, Mount Kuring-gai, NSW 2080, Australia
Distributed in all other territories by Grantham Book Services Ltd.
Isaac Newton Way, Alma Park Industrial Estate, Grantham,
Lincolnshire, NG31 9SD England

Editorial direction by Ghislaine Bavoillot
Book design by Marc Walter

U.S. edition edited by Mary Kalamaras
English translation by Rhona Poritzky Lauvand

Library of Congress Cataloging-in-Publication Data:

Vergé, Roger, 1930–
[Tables de mon moulin. English]
Roger Vergé's new entertaining in the French style / by Roger
Vergé ; photographs by Pierre Hussenot ; styling by Laurence Mouton ;
recipe editing by Adeline Brousse.   p.   cm.
Translation of the rev. ed. originally published: Fêtes maison.
Includes Index
ISBN 1-55670-624-3  (hardcover)
1. Cookery, French. 2. Entertaining.  I. Brousse, Adeline.
II. Vergé, Roger, 1930–  Fêtes maison. III. Title.
TX719.V4815 1997
641.5944--dc21                                    97-12776
                                                         CIP

10 9 8 7 6 5 4 3 2 1

# Roger Vergé's

~

# New Entertaining in the French Style

~

Photography
by Pierre Hussenot

Food Styling
by Laurence Mouton

in Collaboration with
Adeline Brousse

Stewart, Tabori & Chang
~
New York

~ 7 ~

INTRODUCTION

~ 9 ~

BEFORE THE FEAST

~ 31 ~

THE HERBS OF PROVENCE

~ 43 ~

A LUNCHEON
UNDER THE ARBOR

~ 55 ~

TUTTI FRUTTI

~ 65 ~

IN THE HOLIDAY MOOD

~ 75 ~

A LUNCHEON OF FLOWERS

~ 87 ~

A PARTY MENU

~ 101 ~

DINNER AT THE MOUGINS

~ 109 ~

AUNT CÉLESTINE'S
DINNER

~ 119 ~

A SPRING FEAST

~ 129 ~

SCENTS AND SPICES

~ 137 ~

A MENU FOR CLOSE FRIENDS

~ 143 ~

AN AUTUMN LUNCHEON

~ 152 ~

INDEX

~ 159 ~

ACKNOWLEDGMENTS

# EVERY DAY IS A FEAST AT THE MOULIN

~

It has been nearly ten years since I took the readers of my book *Entertaining in the French Style* in a ronde of menus so they could partake in my taste for feasting. In it I offered tips and recipes that enabled them to entertain all year long, for all occasions. I confess that these menus, written according to my own appetite, might be judged as rather copious and the recipes a bit long, but I like to offer a lot of detail. My readers loved the abundance and very warmly welcomed the book both in France and in the United States. But alas times have changed, and readers are pressed to find books that are less imposing as well as less expensive. They worry more and more about their figures and are content with three-course menus, even for celebrations.

It was therefore time to rework the classic *Entertaining in the French Style* according to today's tastes. This new edition is not an abridged version but rather a revision, offering lighter menus with a selection of recipes that, above all, maintains the accent of my cuisine, the *cuisine du soleil* (roughly, cuisine of the sun). I have removed certain menus and modified others. But true gourmands will still find the flavors, fragrances, and joy at the table to which I invite them to share without delay.

I have chosen twelve of my most accessible menus, each illustrating my love for cooking. They will offer you access to the pleasures of the culinary arts. I carefully developed these dishes, always using products available in quantity and quality within each season. I will accompany you step-by-step in the preparation of each dish, while I whisper the thousand small tips that stem from my experience as a chef to help things go more smoothly.

Cooking is an everyday festivity. But more than that, a meal between friends, even a simple family lunch, can turn into something magical. The warmth and friendship that flows around a table celebrates, better than a ceremony, the big as well as the small events.

Let's share together in the pleasures of cooking and creating these privileged moments.

# AVANT LA FÊTE
## (BEFORE THE FEAST)

~

To extend an invitation to partake in a meal is to make a promise to instill in your guests' spirits a symphony of pleasures, both gustative and visual, and perhaps even emotional.

But good recipes alone are not enough to succeed. The attention and passion you put into choosing the food, wines, and table settings will influence the final result. The sensitivity of your efforts will reveal the friendship and love you have for your guests. The setting can be the most essential aspect, and the feast of the tastebuds that follows is that much more brilliant when it comes from the heart.

The advice that follows has two goals: To help you take more pleasure in cooking, and to teach you how to simplify your life—for being available at the moment of serving contributes to the happiness of all.

### SHOPPING

All that the best cooking can do is show off the riches of nature to their advantage. Therefore, success begins with shopping.

The most fortunate find their vegetables in the garden. Nothing equals the flavor of freshly picked fruits, vegetables, and herbs. This is why I grow an abundance of aromatic herbs behind my restaurant, Le Moulin.

They attest to the best memories I have of my uncle. He took care of his vegetable garden according to an unchanging ritual adapted to each harvest. He would never pick a lettuce without first bleaching it by the sun; one week before a lettuce was ready to be picked, he wrapped the outer leaves around the heart and tied them in place with a strand of straw so that, deprived of sunlight, the lettuce whitened in the sun. He never picked a carrot past a certain size, and he abandoned green beans and peas after the third picking, except to give them to the rabbits. "They become tough after the third picking," he said. Flowers, fruits, or vegetables could not, for any reason, be picked

*Regardless of kir's Burgundy origins, why not serve it with a white Provençal wine and nibble on olives from our region as well.*

*Bite into superb, freshly picked raw vegetables, and try them with an anchoïade dip made with anchovy fillets, olive oil, garlic, pastis (anise liquor), mustard, lemon, herbs (thyme, basil, parsley), and pepper. The mixture is blended into a purée in a food processor for a robust concentration of Provence (following double page).*

after the sun had fully risen!

If you don't have a garden, it is sufficient to know how to shop well. I had the good fortune of learning this art from childhood, and perhaps this is how I found my vocation as a chef. Every Friday, Aunt Célestine took me out of school and brought me to the market; actually, it seemed more like a vacation or voyage. I always felt that I was a much better student in this school than in the other.

We began with a general look around, an apparent stroll during which my aunt seemed to content herself with casting an indifferent glance at the farmers' baskets. But when the tour was completed, her mind was made up. Then, with a vaguely interested air, she stopped before the chosen farmer's stand and examined a pair of chickens (back then they were sold in pairs); she verified that the comb was strong, the feet were smooth and white, and the eyes were bright. Then she blew a breath of air into the crop feathers and used her thumb to hold them apart and check that the skin was thin, shiny, and free of any whitish film. She checked that the gizzard wasn't full of grain, which would augment the weight unnecessarily: "Why should I pay for grain that wouldn't benefit either the chicken or myself?" Lastly, she verified that the other chicken that made up the pair was of the same quality as its grain-fed sister.

At the conclusion of these examinations, my aunt's face expressed sorry skepticism, and the farmer, who observed her through the corner of her eye, began to say to herself that she was faced with a tough customer.

"My little woman," the farmer protested (Aunt Célestine was a little woman of more than 220 pounds), "these chickens have eaten nothing but grain. It has been a good week since they no longer range and since I put them in the épinette" (a wicker cage used for fattening chickens in the dark).

"My poor woman," my aunt responded with great pity and perfect insincerity, "your chickens merited to stay one or two more weeks in the épinette. All the same, I cannot put these poor creatures, that are nothing more than skin and bones, on my table." That said, she started on a false exit, knowing that the farmer would hasten to call out to her. This was all part of an immutable ritual, almost a polite gesture, without which the negotiation would not have been of any interest.

Aunt Célestine then announced a firm and definite price that she would not exceed for anything in the world. It was a question of dignity. Moreover, her price was fair, though this did not prevent the farmer from feigning despair on principle. Magnanimously, my aunt then took, at the same price, two or three more pairs of chickens. The farmer, just to get in the last word, exclaimed, "Go ahead! But only because it's for you—though I'm really losing here." This never deceived anyone, but constituted the obligatory and logical ending to the whole transaction.

After the chickens, we bought eggs, a normal progression. Aunt Célestine only accepted brown-shelled eggs; she said the egg yolks were brighter. Then we went on to the cheeses, where the grain and texture revealed if the milk had been heated to the proper temperature and had been properly skimmed. When it came to the butter, it could not be too yellow, which would indicate that the cows had grazed on too many buttercups ("It's pretty to look at, but it takes away from the finesse"), or that it had been rinsed with carrot juice. A small piece broken off with the thumbnail was enough to denounce a butter that had not been rinsed with well water, was poorly pressed, or contained buttermilk.

Oh, to think back to those stories of the good old times, while now neither the epoch nor the markets are the same anymore. However, I assure you that

*The markets in Provence still resemble the one from a song: There we find perfectly fresh tender young vegetables.*

*Ultra-fresh fava beans, peppers, and tomatoes from the Forville market in Cannes.*

we can still find good products with a little effort. The most important thing is to want to take the time and to find pleasure in doing so.

Perfect freshness surpasses all other requirements; never hesitate to replace a doubtful turbot with a less prestigious but freshly caught cod.

At the risk of contradicting the purists, canned and frozen foods, though without a doubt not as good as fresh produce, are better than those that have been displayed on the stand for too long; with a bit of fresh herb or a beautiful tomato, they can create a delightful meal. More importantly, they make available such off-season vegetables as asparagus and peas, canned fruits in syrup, frozen strawberries for coulis (fruit sauces), and raspberries. Fish and shellfish lose some of their flavor and texture when frozen, but can offer suitable results.

Purchase **meat, fowl,** and **game** the day before they are to be used. Wrap them in plastic film so they do not pick up odors from other products in the refrigerator.

**Fish,** especially fillets, should be stored flat; by folding them you risk damaging the flesh. Wrap them as indicated for meat, above, and store them in the coldest section of the refrigerator for no more than twenty-four hours.

**Shellfish** should be alive until the moment it is prepared. You can store live rock lobster or lobster tightly wrapped in newspaper in the refrigerator, below 50°F (10°C), for up to two days.

**Oysters** are also stored in the coldest area of the refrigerator, below 50°F (10°C), for up to eight days after the date they were harvested. Bivalves and mollusks do not keep as long.

**Fruits** and **vegetables** should be cleaned and put away in the vegetable bin of the refrigerator. They should not be stored in an area that is too cold or overly ventilated, as this will cause them to dehydrate. Do not store for more than two or three days.

**Cheeses** should not be purchased far in advance. Treat them carefully, do not throw them into the shopping cart as you would a package of sugar. It takes an experienced cheese merchant to suggest a fine, perfectly matured cheese meant to be eaten at its peak. Leave cheeses separately wrapped in their original paper or in plastic film. Store them in the least cold section of the refrigerator.

**Milk products,** including butter, milk, cream, etc., quickly absorb odors from other foods. They should therefore be well-wrapped or covered.

**Wines** should rest for at least two days (one week for older wines) after being transported, so do not purchase wine at the last moment. Refer to the wine section (below) for the best way to serve them.

Buy **bread** on the same day as the meal; an exception can be made for large country breads or whole-wheat breads, which freeze well. Take them out of the freezer at least an hour in advance. If you should forget to do so, defrost the bread in a moderate oven for ten minutes.

Finally, when shopping, don't forget the little details that give a meal its charm: Candles, flowers, coffee, liqueurs, herb teas, cigars, menus, and small gifts on appropriate occasions.

## WINE

The sensual world of wine is so vast and complex that it can hardly be summed up in a few pages. Possessing this knowledge, my sommelier, Gérard Voisin, knows how to propose bottles that my guests will love, even neophytes, owing to the simple and precise details that he takes care of. But for our purposes it is sufficient to establish a few reference points so that you can choose, marry (match the appropriate wine to the food), and serve wine, without attempting to master this long and difficult, though passionate, domain.

At the end of each recipe, under the rubric "Wine suggestions," I will recommend wines that best harmonize with each dish. By respecting the brief advice below, you will acquire an immense pleasure for wines.

### *The Good Years*

The labels on great wines are always marked with the *millésime*—that is to say the year they were made. There are both stellar and average years, and the chart on page 17 will show you their worldwide reputation. With wines, the exception is often the rule. It is possible that you will find a very good bottle from a modest year, or come across a botched sample from a glorious year. Do not consider this a grave inconvenience, but rather as the eternal confirmation that every wine remains the child of the wine grower, each of whom utilizes his or her own particular knowledge, ideas, and obsessions, often with formidable talent, but sometimes faced with bad luck. Wine is also subject to its own capricious nature; a particular year may be remarkable for one vineyard but mediocre for another situated only a few acres away. The wine chart is merely meant to indicate averages.

If you have confidence in your wine merchant, you will know what to expect from the bottle before opening it. If you buy your wine on your own, taste the wine when possible, before purchasing several bottles. And if you are not a great taster, simply ask yourself if you truly find the wine pleasing. If not, take another.

Finally, remember that just because a wine is considered great it is not necessarily the best choice to accompany all dishes. It is better to serve a less dense Bordeaux from a moderate year to accompany a delicate dish rather than defeat it. As in this case, it may occur to you to expressly choose a wine from a less prestigious year for a marriage of more equilibrium.

*Though from different regions, roquefort cheese and red Hermitage originate from the same arid and windy terrain and therefore marry well.*

# Wine Vintage Chart

Average: *  Good: **  Very Good to Exceptional: ***

<table>
<tr><td>Alsace</td><td>45***, 47***, 49***, 59***, 61***, 64***, 71***, 73***, 74**, 75**, 76***, 77*, 78**, 79**, 81**, 82**, 83***, 84**, 85***, 86*, 87**, 88***, 89***, 90***, 91*, 92**, 93**, 94*, 95*</td></tr>
</table>

**Beaujolais**

Beaujolais Nouveau, Beaujolais and Beaujolais Villages are drunk within a few months following harvest.

The ten vineyards (*crus*): Juliénas, Chenas, Chiroubles, Saint-Amour, Morgon, Fleurie, Brouilly, Côtes-de-Brouilly, Moulin-à-Vent, Régnié.

83**, 85***, 86*, 88**, 89***, 90**, 91***, 92*, 93*, 94*, 95**

**Bordeaux**

Dry whites
70***, 71***, 75***, 76**, 78***, 79**, 80**, 81**, 82***, 83**, 84**, 85***, 86**, 87**, 88***, 89***, 90***, 91*, 92**, 93**, 94**, 95**

Sweet Whites
45***, 47***, 53**, 55**, 59**, 61***, 62**, 64*, 66**, 67***, 69*, 70***, 71***, 75***, 76***, 78***, 79**, 80**, 81**, 82**, 83**, 84*, 85**, 86***, 87*, 88***, 89***, 90***, 91**, 92*, 93*, 94***, 95***

Reds
45***, 47***, 49***, 53***, 55***, 59***, 61***, 62**, 64**, 66***, 69*, 70***, 71**, 75***, 76**, 78***, 79**, 80*, 81**, 82***, 83***, 84*, 85***, 86***, 87**, 88***, 89***, 90***, 91*, 92*, 93*, 94**, 95***

**Burgundy**

Whites
47**, 49**, 53**, 55**, 59**, 61**, 62**, 64**, 66**, 69**, 70**, 71***, 73**, 76**, 78***, 79**, 80*, 81**, 82**, 83**, 84**, 85***, 86**, 87*, 88**, 89***, 90***, 91*, 92**, 93**, 94**, 95**

Reds
45***, 47***, 49***, 53**, 55**, 59***, 61***, 64**, 66**, 69**, 70*, 71***, 76**, 78***, 79**, 80*, 81**, 82**, 83***, 84*, 85***, 86**, 87*, 88***, 89***, 90***, 91**, 92*, 93**, 94**, 95***

<table>
<tr><td>Champagne</td><td>45***, 47***, 60***, 61***, 71**, 73***, 75***, 76**, 78**, 79**, 81**, 82**, 83**, 85***, 86*, 87*, 88**, 89***, 90***, 91*, 92*, 93*, 94**, 95**</td></tr>
</table>

**Côtes-du-Rhône**

Rosés
These wines generally keep only for one or two years.

Whites
78***, 79**, 81*, 82**, 83**, 85**, 86**, 87**, 88**, 89**, 90***, 91**, 92*, 93*, 94**, 95**

Reds
45**, 46**, 47**, 49**, 50**, 53**, 55**, 61**, 62**, 64**, 66**, 67**, 69**, 70**, 71**, 76**, 78***, 79**, 80**, 81**, 82*, 83**, 84*, 85**, 86**, 87*, 88***, 89**, 90***, 91**, 92*, 93*, 94**, 95***

**Loire Valley**

Dry Whites
These wines generally keep only for two or three years, but the exceptions listed here are well worth it.
88***, 89***, 90***, 91*, 92*, 93*, 94**, 95***

Medium whites
70**, 71**, 75**, 76***, 78**, 79**, 81**, 82***, 83***, 85***, 86***, 87**, 88***, 89***, 90***, 91*, 92*, 93*, 94**, 95***

Reds
47***, 59***, 78***, 79**, 80*, 81**, 82***, 83***, 84*, 85***, 86**, 87*, 88***, 89***, 90***, 91*, 92*, 93*, 94**, 95***

<table>
<tr><td>Languedoc-Roussillon</td><td>86**, 88***, 89***, 90***, 91**, 92*, 93*, 94**, 95***</td></tr>
</table>

<table>
<tr><td>Southwest</td><td>70***, 71***, 75***, 76**, 78***, 79**, 82***, 83***, 84*, 85***, 86**, 87*, 88***, 89***, 90***, 92*, 93*, 94**, 95**</td></tr>
</table>

<table>
<tr><td>Provence</td><td>82***, 83**, 85***, 86**, 87**, 88***, 89**, 90***, 91*, 92*, 93*, 94**, 95***</td></tr>
</table>

Certain years are missing from this chart because, in theory, wines from those years do not merit purchasing or drinking. On the other hand, I have listed some very old vintages you probably never will get to taste, but which are so strongly stamped in our eonological culture that they are always fitting to mention.

### Young or Old?

Though no one has ever seen a poor wine develop into a great wine through aging, the destiny of an exceptional bottle will always harbor an unknown side. One bottle may achieve perfect harmony, while a twin bottle has shamelessly decomposed.

Aging depends on the cork, the neck of the bottle, how the wine is stored, and on the smallest incident that may have occurred at the time the wine was bottled, including, I am tempted to say, which way the wind was blowing. In short, the longer you wait the more likely the wine could become outstanding, but the greater risk you take.

In principle, rosés are tasted within the year they are bottled, as are nouveau wines and light reds. The longevity of white and red wines varies enormously, from several months for a young wine to several decades for a jaune du Jura (the golden yellow wines from the Jura region). Wines from great years certainly last longer than those from inferior years.

It was once thought that champagnes should be drunk within the year they were bottled and in general, they deliver their best in the prime of their youth. Therefore, drink the brut non-vintage champagnes upon purchase. But exceptions can be made for vintage bruts, which evolve beautifully up to their sixth and seventh year. Great vintages retain their elegant qualities for a good dozen years.

Inform yourself either through your wine merchant (choose a perfectionist) or the wine grower at the time of purchase.

### How to Store Wine for an Extended Period

The dream of all wine lovers is to have a real underground wine cellar. If you are so fortunate, certain requirements must be respected:

—Maintain a fairly constant temperature ranging from 46.5–55.5°F (8–13°C), without drastic variations.

—Darkness is obligatory.

—Maintain high humidity (70–90%) to prevent the corks from drying out and to contribute to a stable temperature. It is better to have a wine cellar that is too humid than too dry; don't worry if the wine labels fall to pieces, the wine will not suffer.

—Vibrations, and odors from paint cans, onions, old cartons covered with

*This traditional ornamental figure of a little grape picker laden with raisins brings to life, in miniature, an old Provençal metier (trade).*

mildew, etc., are to be avoided. Therefore, do not store bottles in their cartons. —Wine bottles should never be set upright. Store bottles flat on their sides so the wine remains in contact with the cork. This will limit the small exchanges between the air in the bottle and the air in the wine cellar that passes through the cork.

## The Art of Serving Wine

If you only own one piece of equipment for serving wine it should be a thermometer. The greatest vintage could resemble swill if it is served too warm; the most fragrant Beaujolais loses all its aroma if iced. Below 41°F (5°C), you may as well drink something else; above 64.5°F (18°C) it would be better to drink a grog. Wine detests excessive temperatures.

**How to chill wine.** The wine cellar is the best place, although it is rarely cooler than 50°F (10°C). To obtain lower temperatures use an ice bucket; first put the wine bottle in the bucket, fill the bucket half-full with cold water, and finish by adding ice cubes. Chilling wine in a refrigerator makes it more difficult to control the temperature and takes longer than an ice bucket.

**How to *chambre* or bring a wine to room temperature.** The term *chambre* means to bring the wine to room temperature, i.e., the temperature of the room in which the wine is to be drunk. The expression goes back to the time when people lived in rooms that were heated to no more than 60°F

*A light, fruity wine served chilled makes a good summery apéritif. The palate will be better prepared for the meal if the wine can also be savored with the first course.*

(16°C). Bringing a wine to room temperature in a 68°F (20°C) kitchen will yield disastrous results. Therefore, we no longer truly chambre a wine, but rather gently warm it to 60°F (16°C). Never, in any case, place a bottle near a heat source such as a radiator or chimney.

Always serve the wine 2–4°F (1–2°C) below the ideal drinking temperature, as wine is never drunk in one gulp and warms up once it is in the glass. This way you can avoid it becoming too warm before you have the chance to savor it.

## Correct Serving Temperatures for Wine

| | | |
|---|---|---|
| ALSACE | | Chilled, 48–52°F (9–11°C) |
| BEAUJOLAIS | Beaujolais, B. Villages, or B. Nouveau | Chilled, 50–54°F (10–12°C) |
| | Ten vineyards | 57–59° (14–15 °C) |
| BORDEAUX | Dry whites | Chilled, 50–52°F (10–11°C) |
| | Sweet whites | Iced, 45–48°F (7–9°C) |
| | Reds | Chambrés, 61–65°F (16–18°C) |
| BURGUNDY | Whites | Fairly chilled, 54–56°F (12–13°C) |
| | Reds | 57–61°F (14–16 °C) |
| CHAMPAGNE | | Chilled, 46–50°F (8–10°C) |
| CÔTES-DU-RHÔNE | Rosés | Chilled, 46–50°F (8–10°C) |
| | Whites | 54–57°F (12–14°C) |
| | Reds | Chambrés, 61–63°F (16–17°C) |
| LOIRE VALLEY | Dry whites | Chilled, 48–50°F (9–10°C) |
| | Sweet whites | Iced, 46–50°F (8–9°C) |
| | Rosés | Well chilled, 43–46°F (6–8°C) |
| | Reds | 56–59°F (13–15°C) |
| PROVENCE | Whites and rosés | Iced, 45–48°F (7–9°C) |
| | Reds | Chambrés, 61–63°F (15–17°C) |
| SOUTHWEST | Red | Chambrés, 61–63°F (16–17°C) |
| LANGUEDOC-ROUSSILLON | Whites and rosés | Iced, 45–48°F (7–9°C) |
| | Reds | 57–63°F (14–17°C) |

**Bottle or carafe?** Whenever possible, serve wine in its bottle. It is easier, and guests enjoy reading the label to see what they are drinking.

Very old wines must breathe before they are served. Pour them into a carafe to oxygenate them for no more than a few minutes before serving. They are fragile and become stale soon after having had a boost of oxygen.

Very young wines must breathe if they are a bit high in alcohol or carbon dioxide; breathing lightens them before they reach the glass.

Today's wines are almost always filtered and produce very little sediment with age so decanting is not required. If you should happen upon an old bottle in which the sediment will assail the limpidity of the wine, pour the wine slowly and gently in front of a light source so that it flows against the inside rim of the carafe. Stop pouring as soon any sediment appears.

**When to uncork a bottle?** The rules are the same as for serving wine in a carafe. Actually, it is rare that you need to complicate matters by opening a bottle far in advance. Most importantly, you should taste the wine before serving the food to verify that there aren't any major defects, such as the wine being corked (having taken on an odor or flavor of the cork), so you can replace the bottle if necessary. After you taste the wine, it will benefit from being recorked to prevent it from oxidizing too quickly. If a wine is only slightly corked decant it, and with a little luck the shot of air will bring it back into shape.

**The wine basket.** This is attractive, but slightly outdated. If the sediment is terribly bothersome, decant the wine as indicated above. The important thing to remember is that a very old wine that has sediment should be returned to the vertical position very gradually (doing this in successive positions can take up to one hour). To prevent the sediment from mixing with the wine, you won't be able to decant after it is set upright.

**The corkscrew.** Good wines have very long corks. The corkscrew should have a screw long enough to go through the entire length of the cork without damaging it. The threading should be smooth (without a sharp edge) and, if possible, covered with a nonstick coating. Pull the cork out smoothly and gradually. Trinket-type corkscrews should always be avoided.

Do not imitate bistro waiters by holding the bottle between the knees when opening it; this method is not very elegant, and if there is any sediment it will mix with the wine. If a wine has a leaky cork, open the bottle as soon as possible and drink it.

As for champagne, at the risk of losing your reputation as the life of the party, never pop the cork loudly. Hold the bottle at an angle and slowly pull out the cork, keeping a hold on it just at the moment when it is about to pop out. This will prevent the foam from overflowing, as long as the champagne was properly chilled and the bottle was not shaken just before being opened.

**Glasses.** Although each wine region has its own special shape, there is no dictate for using them. However, wine does taste best in a stemmed glass. Hold the glass by the stem, never by the sides of the glass itself; otherwise, after two or three sips, you will no longer see the color of the wine through the streaks and fingerprints.

The glass should be wide at the middle and taper slightly toward the rim. Only fill the glass one-third full so that the surface of the wine reaches the widest point of the glass. You should be able to swirl the wine in the glass (without splashing it on your clothing) to better release the wine's aroma, which remains at the top of the glass; concentrated there, it will escape less quickly due to the tapered rim, allowing you time to savor the pleasure.

Quality glass such as crystal is recommended.

## CHEESE

France has the privilege of being the producer of over four hundred varieties of cheese. And—with an even greater privilege—France is able to offer farm cheeses made from raw milk. A "living" cheese evolves, matures, and ripens as a beautiful fruit does. The fabrication of cheese requires a great deal of knowledge and passion on the part of both the farmer and the *affineur*—the person who finishes the cheese (by ripening and bringing them to maturity). To better understand the magnificence of a cheese it is helpful to observe my friends Édouard and Robert Ceneri of the Ferme Savoyarde in Cannes.

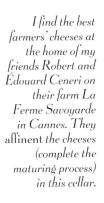

*I find the best farmers' cheeses at the home of my friends Robert and Édouard Ceneri on their farm La Ferme Savoyarde in Cannes. They* affinent *the cheeses (complete the maturing process) in this cellar.*

*My Aunt Célestine ripened and matured her cheeses in a garde-manger, or cheese cabinet, which is well aerated and kept in a dark area. The wire-mesh door protects the cheeses from insects.*

They follow the evolution of their "crop," which is sold throughout France. They speak about their cheeses with words they invented for themselves and which resemble words of love.

On the other hand, do not expect anything from cheeses stamped *laiters* (commercially made cheeses), which are made with either raw or pasteurized milk. These cheeses are tasteless; their flavor is determined forever at the factory, and they will only depreciate in time—if it is possible for them to lose any flavor.

In my opinion, cheeses must be served with bread such as toasted country bread, walnut bread, or raisin bread, and never with crackers. They can be eaten with salad with a dressing very light in vinegar, and even with certain fruits and nuts such as apples, pears, grapes, and walnuts. For example, serve a Williams pear with a vacherin cheese—and tell me what you think!

Take the cheeses out of the refrigerator at least thirty minutes before serving, keeping them wrapped. They should be eaten at slightly below room temperature. It is best to place the cheeses on a platter just before serving. If you prefer to prepare a cheese platter in advance, cover it with plastic film or a lightly moistened kitchen towel.

Design a cheese platter so that there is something for everyone; goat cheese, cow cheese, sheep cheese, and blue cheese. Choose cheeses with a variety of textures; firm and soft, fresh and dry.

## FLOWERS

The art of flower arranging is similar to the art of cooking: We have the same supplier—the sun—and the products for both are taken from the garden.

My wife, Denise, skillfully arranges the decorations for the Moulin de Mougins. She has made bouquets that include sprigs of aromatic plants such as pink flowering thyme, white flowering savory, and rosemary's blue corolla. These "edible" fragrances waft over the tables.

She also uses luminous bay leaves, velvety sage, mint and basil for their perfume, tarragon for its rampant foliage, and olive and other fruit-tree branches, with, when possible, their fruits or flowers, such as orange, hazelnut with pussy willows or nuts, verbena, creeping ivy, oak with acorns, and chestnut with burrs. Give yourself the freedom to follow your imagination and make each bouquet with a bit of self-expression. Daisies picked by a child are usually more beautiful than an expensive orchid.

There are a few rules to follow: Avoid flowers with heady aromas such as tuberoses, unless the table is very large and the bouquet is far from your guests' noses. Avoid very large or tall bouquets that will transform conversations into a game of hide-and-seek. If the bouquets are considerable, it is best to use very straight tall vases that will allow your guests to see each other.

Try to harmonize the flowers with the theme of your meal; if it is springtime, wild flowers are preferable to a bouquet of roses.

If the table is too small for flowers, place the bouquet on a sideboard or a piece of nearby furniture, or more simply, place a single flower on the tablecloth above each plate or on each napkin.

*My wife, Denise, finds her inspiration in the garden. She arranges the bouquets for our two restaurants, the Moulin de Mougins and the Amandier.*

## MUSIC

Music is the final touch in setting the scene, on the condition that it is not so deafeningly loud that it will get in the way of conversation. The choice should please all guests; classical music or jazz are, in general, unanimously appreciated, so try not to stray too far from these.

### COFFEE AND ACCOMPANIMENTS AT THE END OF THE MEAL

The moment for coffee should not be neglected. Never forget to offer it, and continue to follow the high standards you have given the entire meal up to that point. Carefully choose appropriate accompaniments: Eaux-de-vie brandies, liqueurs, cigars, and even chocolates.

Prepare everything in advance on a platter: Cups, saucers, spoons, coffee pot, creamer, cocktail-sized napkins, and sugar bowl. Granulated sugar is preferable to sugar cubes to keep the cream from "breaking up." Most importantly, don't overly sweeten your coffee; the most delicate and aromatic brews do very well without sugar.

Place the liqueur glasses and bottles on a second platter. Keep the clear liquors and their glasses in the refrigerator or freezer up to the last moment.

When a bottle of liquor is opened for the first time, allow it to aerate for several hours before drinking in order to dissipate the ether vapors that can sting the eyes and nose. Also prepare the cigar box, cigar-cutter, matches, and ashtrays.

But, above all, do not prepare the coffee. Wait until the last moment or the aroma will evaporate. Don't forget to warm the coffee pot by rinsing it with boiling hot water before filling it with coffee.

Don't hesitate to awaken the end of the meal by offering an unusual coffee. Here are a few recipes:

### *Café Brûlot*

For 6 servings: In a food processor fitted with the blade attachment, grind ½ stick of cinnamon, 6 whole cloves, the zest of 1 lemon and 1 orange cut into thin strips, and 3 sugar cubes. Combine this mixture with 4 oz (120 ml) fine cognac and 2 tablespoons (30 ml) curaçao in a small saucepan and place over high heat. As soon as the liquor starts to simmer, flambé (do this at a distance from the exhaust hood to prevent the filter from catching fire), while stirring with a very long spoon until the sugar has dissolved. Gradually

*The ingredients for a Café Brûlot surround a cup designed by Jean Dufy in 1921.*

pour in a generous pint (500ml) of very strong, hot coffee and continue to stir the mixture until the flame goes out.

*This Café Brûlot has been made famous by Brennan's, a restaurant in New Orleans. The founder's grandson spent three months in the kitchens at the Moulin de Mougins and showed me the secret of its preparation.

## Café Royal

Single serving: Sprinkle a small plate with a layer of confectioners' sugar. Prepare the coffee. Rub the inner, white side of a strip of lemon zest around the border of a thick glass. Turn the glass over and set it upside down in the confectioners' sugar so that the sugar adheres to the lightly moistened rim. Turn the glass upright and squeeze 2 more strips of lemon zest into the glass to release a few droplets of its oil, then drop the zest into the glass. Place a spoon in the glass to prevent it from cracking from the heat.

In a small ladle, heat 4 tablespoons of cognac over a flame. Pour the cognac into the glass and flambé. As soon as the flame goes out pour in the hot coffee. Serve immediately.

## Irish Coffee

Single serving: Place 2 sugar cubes in a thick stemmed glass. Fill the glass to ½ inch (1.3 cm) from the rim with very hot black coffee. Add 2–3 tablespoons whiskey, stir. Delicately pour lightly whipped cream over the back of a spoon so it stays on top of the coffee without sinking in.

## Café "Bistouille"

Single serving: Place 1 sugar cube and 1 pinch of powdered cinnamon in a warmed coffee cup. Add 2 tablespoons of marc or Calvados. Fill with hot coffee. Serve immediately.

### COOKING AND CHILDREN

We often complain about the way children eat today and we deplore the fact that their palates are not educated. So above all, do not chase them out of the kitchen! I very much enjoy cooking with my daughter, Cordélia, now eighteen. Since she was very young she always took pleasure in being with me in the kitchen and I made the most of it for her so she would hold onto this joyful passion. We invented dishes together. I created dishes for her according to her tastes and appetite, and she dreamed up dishes for me and gave me judicious suggestions.

Cordélia adores making pastries. Moreover, she confided in me when she was five or six years old that she wanted to become a pastry chef. One day when she was making tartlets, after the dough had been perfectly shaped into each little mold, I saw her brushing the dough with honey, then sprinkling sugar on top. I asked her why she put the honey on before the sugar. Surprised by my ignorance, she replied, "Goodness, it's to hold the sugar in place." Logical, isn't it?

Therefore, give children a part of the responsibility. Later on, you will be happy you did. In the past, the family lived in one room near the hearth where the cauldron was simmering. Traditions and recipes were passed on from generation to generation. All young girls knew how to prepare a soup, a stew, or a tart. Although I was obviously never a young girl, it is to this tradition and to my Aunt Célestine that I owe my vocation as a chef. On my fifth birthday my aunt bought me a small bench on which I could hoist myself up to see what was simmering in the pots. I didn't help her much, and no doubt I got in her way a bit, but she knew that this was the way she could help me discover the marvelous world of cooking. So provide your children with a thousand little tasks that will make them proud to help you in the kitchen, and when they are adults their good taste will already be formed.

# LES HERBES DE PROVENCE
## (THE HERBS OF PROVENCE)

~

*La soupe à la farigoulette*
*(Artichoke and Wild Thyme Soup)*

*La fricassée de moules au fenouil*
*(Mussels and Fennel in Saffron Cream Sauce)*

*La glace à la lavande avec les petits pains d'anis*
*(Lavender Ice Cream with Small Anise Cookies)*

~

*The morning picking in the garrigue and the garden yields a harvest of wild fragrances that will heighten the cooking.*

While on my walks in the Provençal countryside, I have the habit of brushing my hands against the herbs in front of me as I pass. Sometimes I break off a stem and push it deep into my pocket. Rosemary, savory, fennel, lavender; they secretly make up rich scented bouquets. I dig my hand into the bottom of my pocket and rub the herb stems together, then breathe in the perfume on my skin. This scent brings me very close to the soil I love; I have the impression of merging with it, of possessing it.

Once, a few lavender flowers became stuck to a honey candy I had forgotten in my pocket. I gently sucked on this find, and the aroma that swept through my nose and mouth was very much like happiness itself. This is how the idea of flavoring luscious lavender ice cream with honey came to me, and I wish to share the recipe with you here.

It sometimes occurs to me to put a fistful of these wild herbs in my dishes, such as the *farigoulette* soup. This is what we call the wild thyme that abounds in the Provence *garrigues*. When you smell it, you can hear the cicadas sing.

I learned how to breathe in the vegetation in search of new pleasures, so along with my passion for mother-of-thyme, sage, mint, marjoram, bay leaf, or basil, I have developed more unusual interests. For example, have you ever

placed your nose on olive or fig leaves? Allow yourself to be taken away by
the leaves that bloom at the same time as the wild figs set in the middle tuft of
each branch. These are the ones that should be picked. The next time you
roast an exceptional chicken in a heavy cast-iron casserole, first allow it to
brown, then cover it with these tender leaves. Put the lid on the casserole,
lower the oven, and slowly finish cooking. When you taste it you will understand what I am talking about.

**For the apéritif:** This appealing orange wine punch is a traditional Provençal apéritif that goes well with any meal from our region. The fragrant spices
herald this herb-based menu. In a large glass jar put 2 quartered bitter
(Seville) oranges, 10 peppercorns, 1 vanilla bean, ½ cinnamon stick, 1 generous quart (1 liter) rosé wine, and 1 cup (250 ml) cognac. Set the punch aside
to macerate for 20 days in a cool, dark area. Add 1 cup (200 g) sugar. Set aside
for 10 more days. Strain and bottle the punch.

# La soupe à la farigoulette
## (Artichoke and Wild Thyme Soup)

~

**Shopping:** *Farigoule* or *farigoulette* is wild thyme. If unavailable, use the freshest common thyme available.

**Several hours in advance:** Cook the artichokes in boiling salted water, 1 tablespoon coarse salt per quart (7 g per liter), for approximately 45 minutes, just until the leaves can be easily pulled off. Begin to check for doneness after 30 minutes.

During this time, cut the baguette into thin slices and toast them.

Finely dice the onion. Heat the oil in a large saucepan. Add the onion and cook until tender over low heat. Do not let the onion brown. When tender, add 1 quart (1 liter) salted water. Turn the heat up to high. At the first boil, add the rice, parsley, and all but 6 thyme sprigs (to be used for decoration). Lower the heat and cook over low heat for about 30 minutes, until the rice is tender.

As soon as the artichokes are cooked, drain them and remove the leaves. Scrape off the flesh from the largest leaves with a spoon. Take advantage of this time to serenely suck on the

Preparation: 25 minutes
Cooking: 50 minutes

Ease: Easy
Cost: Economical
Yield: 6 servings

Ingredients:
2 large artichokes or
5 small violet artichokes
½ baguette
1 large white onion
5 tablespoons olive oil
1¾ oz (50 g) short-grain rice
1 bunch flat-leaf parsley,
tied with string
1 bunch *farigoule* or common
thyme, tied with string
1 cup (250 ml) heavy cream,
very cold
Salt and pepper, to taste

Soupe à la farigoulette
(*Artichoke and Wild
Thyme Soup*) surrounded by its raw ingredients
and accompanying
croûtons.

smallest leaves (they are so good) while removing the choke and trimming it off the bottoms. Place the bottoms and the flesh, into the cooked soup. Bring the soup to a boil, remove the parsley and thyme. Purée the soup, either with a food processor or stick blender, to obtain a *velouté*—a creamy, smooth consistency.

Put the heavy cream in a large chilled bowl and whip it either with an electric beater or a hand whisk. Stop as soon as the cream begins to take on very soft peaks.

*If you prepare this soup in advance, store the soup and whipped cream separately in the refrigerator.

**Just before serving:** Bring the soup to a boil. Season with a pinch of salt and grind of pepper. Pour the soup into a soup tureen. Dollop the whipped cream on top. Serve immediately. (Only very lightly blend the soup with a ladle at the table just before serving.)

Serve the toasted baguette slices on the side.

**Wine suggestion:** With soup, it is possible to forego the wine. If you wish to fill your guests' glasses, a white cassis, chilled to 46–50°F (8–10°C), will offer a good marriage of fragrances.

# La fricassée de moules au fenouil
## (Mussels and Fennel with Saffron Cream Sauce)

~

**Shopping:** Purchase the freshest mussels available. They should be firmly closed, so reject any (without pity) that are open. Store them for no more than 24 hours in the refrigerator in the vegetable bin—any colder will kill them.

**Several hours in advance:** Scrub the mussels with a brush and pull off any beards, in 3–4 changes of water. Heat 6 tablespoons of the olive oil in a stockpot, then add the mussels and bouquet garni. Cover and cook for a few minutes over high

For this soup to be exquisite, choose the freshest artichokes available. Personally, I have a weakness for the little violet artichokes from Provence.

A symphony of warm tones brought out by the eggs, saffron, carrot, and red pepper reinforces the appetizing orange mussels. The parsley throws a fresh note over the entire dish (opposite page).

A menu based on Provençal herbs enriches the côtes de veau au pastis (Veal Chops with Anise and Garlic, page 148), served in front of my friend César's house (following double page).

Preparation: 45 minutes

Cooking: 30 minutes


Ease: Easy

Cost: Economical

Yield: 6 servings


Ingredients:

3 1/3 lb (1.5 kg) small orange-
fleshed mussels

9 tablespoons olive oil

1 bouquet garni:

1 sprig thyme, 1 bay leaf,
several sprigs parsley,
all tied together

3 small carrots

1 red bell pepper

1 fennel bulb

6 egg yolks

10 fl oz (300 ml) heavy cream

1 pinch saffron

salt and pepper to taste

3 tablespoons parsley,
coarsely chopped

heat, stirring occasionally. After all the mussels have opened, take the stockpot off the heat.

Peel the carrots. Seed the red pepper and trim off the white pith. Wash the fennel. Cut the vegetables into strips. Heat the vegetables in a sauté pan with the 3 remaining tablespoons olive oil, 6 tablespoons water, and 1 pinch salt. Cook for approximately 10 minutes over high heat, until the water is completely evaporated and the vegetables are done.

During this time, take the mussels out of the stockpot with a slotted spoon, reserving the cooking liquid. Sort the mussels. Separate the two shell halves, place the halves to which the mussels are attached on a serving platter, discard the empty halves and discard any mussels that have not opened. Scatter the cooked vegetables over the mussels. Set aside the sauté pan to finish the sauce (no need to wash it). Cover the mussels and vegetables with a sheet of aluminum foil and set them in an area where they can stay warm, but not hot.

Pour the mussel cooking liquid through a fine mesh strainer into a saucepan. Stop pouring before you reach the end; any sand will have fallen to the bottom of the liquid and should be discarded. Refrigerate.

In a bowl, whisk together the egg yolks, heavy cream, and saffron. Refrigerate.

**Twenty-five minutes before serving:** Preheat the oven to 400°F (200°C). Place the mussels, covered with aluminum foil, in the oven for 10 minutes.

Bring the mussel liquid to a boil over high heat. Pour it into the bowl with the cream mixture, stirring briskly to prevent the egg yolks from curdling. Pour the mixture into the sauté pan the vegetables were cooked in and heat over a low flame, stirring constantly. Do not allow the sauce to boil. As soon as the sauce thickens, take it off the heat. Season with a pinch of salt and a grind of fresh pepper. Pour the sauce over the mussels and vegetables. Sprinkle with parsley. Serve immediately.

**Wine suggestion:** If you served wine with the soup why not continue with the same wine, white cassis? Another option would be an elegant Côtes-du-Rhône such as a white Hermitage, dry but round and full bodied. Chill the wine to 46–50°F (8–10°C), but no colder, or you will mar its spice and dried-fruit fragrance.

## La glace à la lavande avec les petits pains d'anis
### (Lavender Ice Cream with Small Anise Cookies)

~

**Shopping:** *Use fresh or dried lavender, lavender flowers, or lavender sugar (see below), but above all, do not use the lavender (often found in little sacks) intended to perfume clothing, as it contains a perfume base not meant for consumption. †Green anise can be found in specialty stores.

*La glace à la lavande*
*(Lavender Ice Cream)*

**The day before or six hours in advance:** For the lavender sugar: Using a food processor or mortar and pestle, grind the lavender flowers to a fine powder, add the sugar and blend well. Add mixture to the milk, stirring until the sugar is dissolved.

In a bowl, whisk the egg yolks with the heavy cream. Stir in the milk-lavender sugar mixture and pour through a fine-meshed strainer. Pour the mixture into the ice-cream machine. Freeze according to manufacturer's directions.

As soon as the ice cream is set, scoop out 12 balls or ovals with an ice-cream scoop or 12 quenelles with 2 soup spoons dipped in warm water. To make the quenelles, first scoop up a good-sized ball of ice cream with one soup spoon. Place the second soup spoon on top of the ice cream and turn it over to scoop up the ice cream. Repeat this step several times going back and forth from spoon to spoon to form an attractive

Preparation: 50 minutes
Cooking: 15 minutes

Ease: Easy
Cost: Economical
Yield: 6 servings

Ingredients:
*For the ice cream:*
1 teaspoon lavender flowers
1 cup (200 g) sugar
1 cup (250 ml) milk
8 egg yolks
1 cup (250 ml) heavy cream

*For the spice cookies:*
1¾ cup flour
1¼ cup (250 g) sugar
2 teaspoons (10 g) green anise seeds †
1 pinch salt
2 or 3 egg whites
3½ tablespoons (50 g) butter

quenelle. Place two quenelles or scoops of ice cream in an ice-cream goblet or small bowl. Place them in the freezer. Repeat for each serving.

**Just before serving:** Place each goblet or bowl of ice cream on a small plate decorated with a paper doily and a lavender sprig.

**Decorating suggestion:** Freeze the lavender sprigs intended to decorate each plate. Moisten the frozen lavender sprigs in water, then quickly roll them in granulated sugar. Set them aside to dry on a plate of sugar.

**Improvise!** You can replace the sugar in the ice cream with 2 tablespoons of lavender honey.

*Les petits pains d'anis*
*(Small Anise Cookies)*

**The day ahead or several hours in advance:** In a large bowl, combine the flour, sugar, anise seeds, and salt. Whip the egg whites with a fork just until they begin to foam, not to soft peaks.

Pour ⅔ of the beaten egg whites into the flour-sugar mixture and stir to combine. You should obtain the consistency of a slightly thick tart dough. If needed, add a bit more or all of the remaining egg white to reach the proper consistency. The dough should be very sticky. Flour your hands and roll the dough into a ball. Wrap it in plastic film and refrigerate for at least 1 hour.

Preheat the oven to 350°F (180°C). Dust the work surface with flour and roll out the dough ⅓-inch (8 mm) thick. Cut the dough into about 20 ovals, preferably with a cookie cutter. Arrange the ovals on a buttered or nonstick sheet pan.

Decorate the cookies with a chevron design using the tip of a knife. Dust off any excess flour with a pastry brush. Bake for approximately 15 minutes.

With a spatula, transfer the baked cookies from the sheet pan onto a cooling rack. After cooling, arrange the crisp cookies in an airtight container; they can be stored for several days.

**Just before serving:** To complete the presentation for the lavender ice cream, place one anise cookie on each plate. Arrange the remaining cookies on an attractive platter so guests can serve themselves.

**Serving suggestion:** These little anise cookies are delicious with a well-ripened melon. Try it!

# Un Déjeuner sous la Tonnelle
## (A Luncheon Under the Arbor)

~

*La salade de langouste au beurre d'orange*
*(Warm Rock-Lobster Salad with Orange Butter Sauce)*

*La fondue de gigot aux aubergines et la compote niçoise*
*(Lamb and Eggplant Timbales and Niçoise Vegetable Compote)*

*Les crêpes au miel et aux pignons de Provence*
*(Crêpes in Honey with Provençal Pine Nuts)*

~

*The warmth of a gastronomic dream by day: An exceptional meal served in the shade of the trellis where raisins slowly ripen. (Home of Bernard Chevery, who organizes great Cannes gatherings.)*

Le Rendez-vous des Sportifs in Nice is not one of those formal restaurants that attract gastronomes worldwide, or a modern temple of sensationalist cooking. Owner Marinette serves simple, wholesome, flavorful cooking in pantagruelian portions.

Obtaining one of Marinette's recipes is much more complicated than eating one of her dishes. Not that she's trying to protect her secrets, but cooking seems so simple to her that she believes anyone can do it as spontaneously as she does.

For example, this is how she explained to me her recipe for *pissaladiére:* "Oh, that's very easy. Take some tepid water, some olive oil, a little salt, pepper, and a few packets of baker's yeast, you know, the kind that comes in cubes. You also take some flour. You crush the yeast, mix, and—voilà!"

"But, Marinette, what are the quantities for all that?"

She looked at me as though she were asking herself if I was really a cook.

What quantities? She has never weighed or measured an ingredient. She makes food, not mathematics. These big chefs have very funny notions.

And so this is why I know how to make lobster fricassee, but I still don't know how to make *pissaladiére* like Marinette. And I deeply regret it. I make up for it by creating great dishes with the most simple products that release the fragrances of my soil: Eggplant, zucchini, thyme, tomato, artichoke, honey, lamb with the scent of our *maquis* (the fragrance in the air produced by the herbs and foliage). All this is represented in the following menu flavored by the sun.

**For the apéritif:** To properly prepare the palate for all the nuances in this high-flying menu, this my idea of the perfect cocktail to offer: In a beautiful iced glass pitcher, pour 8 tablespoons orange juice, 5 tablespoons orange liqueur, 5 tablespoons sugar syrup, and several drops of Angostura bitters. At the last moment, just before serving, pour in 1 bottle of champagne or dry white wine and add several skinned orange slices.

*Mediterranean crustaceans, herbs, fruits, and vegetables from our region are made to be loved in our cooking.*

# La salade de langouste
## au beurre d'orange
### (Warm Rock-Lobster Salad with Orange Butter Sauce)

~

**Shopping:** *I prefer violet Provençal artichokes. They are eaten when still young and small and the choke has barely developed. Break off the stem level to the base (where the leaves begin). If the artichoke is very fresh it should break off cleanly along with any fibrous strands.

†The mixed salad can be comprised of radicchio, *mâche* (lamb's quarters), chicory, romaine, and escarole. The ideal choice would be to find a real Provençal-style mesclun: A mixture of young, tender leaves of the same lettuces, combined with small leaves of unusual lettuces and herbs such as arugula, chervil, curly endive, purslane, etc.

‡The rock lobster can be replaced with lobster. Either way, it would be in your interest to order them in advance at the fish store. Accept them only if they are alive.

**Several hours in advance:** Bring 1 gallon (4 liters) salted water to boil.

Break off the artichoke stems. Wash the artichokes, then plunge them in the boiling water. Cover and let boil for 20 minutes. Pull on a leaf; it will detach easily when the artichokes are done. If not, continue cooking.

Meanwhile, wash the lettuces.

Bring 1 generous quart (1 liter) water to a boil. Put in the tomatoes for a few seconds. Refresh the tomatoes under cold running water. Peel off the skin. Cut the tomatoes in half crosswise and gently press on each half with your hands to extract the seeds. Cut the peeled, seeded tomatoes into small cubes and set them aside on a large plate.

When the artichokes are cooked, set them upside down so the water can drain off. Pull off the leaves and cut out the chokes. Using a stainless-steel knife, cut the artichoke bottoms

Preparation: 55 minutes
Cooking: 40 minutes

Ease: Somewhat difficult
Cost: Expensive
Yield: 6 servings

Ingredients:
6 small violet artichokes *
3 handfuls mixed lettuce †
3 very ripe medium tomatoes
1 bouquet garnis: 1 bay leaf,
1 thyme sprig, 2 parsley
sprigs, and a few chervil
stems, all tied together
3 rock lobsters or lobsters, ‡
about 1 lb (500 g) each
or 1 large lobster, about
3 lbs (1,500 g)
2 oranges
Salt and pepper, to taste
12 tablespoons (180 g) butter
6 pinches chervil leaves

*This is the way I present the* salade de langouste au beurre d'orange *(Warm Rock-Lobster Salad with Orange Butter Sauce). An inquiring disposition always amplifies the seductive powers of a recipe.*

into thin slices. Set aside on the same plate as the tomatoes.

Heat 1 gallon (4 liters) of generously salted water with the bouquet garni. At the first boil, put in the live lobsters. Cover and continue to boil for 8–10 minutes from the time the water returns to a boil.

Meanwhile, peel the oranges, trimming off the pith and with the skin with a knife (see note below). Cut off 12 sections, sliding a sharp knife along the side of each membrane that separates the sections to the center of the orange. Do this over a bowl to catch the juice and orange sections. Pour the juice into a saucepan. Squeeze the juice from the 2 remaining oranges into the saucepan. Reduce the juice over moderate heat until only 2 tablespoons remain. Set aside, leaving it in the saucepan.

When the lobsters are cooked, separate the heads from the tails. Cut through the thin underside of the tails lengthwise using kitchen shears. Remove the tail meat and cut it into thin slices. Crack the claws and remove the meat as well. Store the rock lobster meat in a cool area, but not in the refrigerator.

**30 minutes before serving:** Preheat the oven to 375°F (190°C). Place the washed, drained, and dried lettuces on 6 slightly warm plates. Arrange the artichoke slices over the lettuces. Scatter the tomato cubes, and place 2 orange sections on each plate. Arrange the rock lobster slices, overlapping them, on top, dividing the meat equally among the plates. Salt and pepper lightly.

Reheat the reduced orange juice. Add the cold butter, cut into small cubes in 3 or 4 batches, briskly whisking over high heat. As soon as the sauce is emulsified, take it off the heat and add a pinch of salt and a grind of pepper.

Place the garnished plates in the oven for 2–3 minutes, just enough to slightly warm all the ingredients. Nap each plates with the hot orange butter and sprinkle with chervil. Serve immediately.

**Chef's tip:** To peel the oranges, first cut off the peel at the top and bottom so the fruit is exposed. Place the orange upright on a cutting board on one of the flat cut ends. Run the knife from top to bottom and cut the skin and pith off in strips, barely cutting against the fruit.

**Improvise!** To make this delicious dish more economical, replace the rock lobster or lobster with dungeness crab, spider crab, or lobsterette (*langoustine*).

**Wine suggestions:** This is the moment to uncork a great white wine. Choose a Hermitage (northern Côtes-du-Rhône) or a Pouilly-Fuissé (Burgundy). Serve the wine well chilled at 47–50°F (8–10°C), but not so cold that it would "break the nose," which is to say, smother the aroma.

## La fondue de gigot aux aubergines
### (Lamb and Eggplant Timbales )

~

Though a bit long, this recipe is a significant part of the Moulin repertoire. Many friends have asked for it. If prepared in advance, it reheats well. Courage, it is well worth it!

**Shopping:** *It doesn't matter whether you use branch celery or root celery, it is the quantity and the freshness that count for a glorious aroma. †For the sauce, use a full-bodied red wine, but one that is not too expensive; for example, a generic Côtes-du-Rhône or Villages appellation.

**The day or morning ahead:** Ask your butcher to bone a leg of lamb without cutting into the meat and to give you, in separate pieces, the 3 cushions or leg muscles (the most attractive pieces), the small trimmings (cleaned of fat and membrane), and the bone. Place the small trimmings and heavy cream in the coldest section of the refrigerator; they should be ice cold

Preparation : 1 hour, 30 minutes
Cooking : 1 hour

Ease: Difficult
Cost: Fairly expensive
Yield: 10 servings

Ingredients:
1 leg of lamb weighing 4½ pounds (2 kg)
10 tablespoons heavy cream, well chilled
1 medium (100 g) onion
2 medium (100 g) carrots
1 celery rib

*(Continued on page 48)*

2 tablespoons vegetable oil

3 garlic cloves

1 bouquet garni: 4–5 parsley sprigs, 3 thyme sprigs, and 2 bay leaves, all tied together

3–4 medium (400 g) tomatoes

Salt and pepper, to taste

2 cups (500 ml) full-bodied red wine †

1 tablespoon cornstarch

1 pinch nutmeg

2 eggplants

4 tablespoons olive oil

*If you have the good luck of finding Cévennes sweet onions, do not hesitate to use them; they have a tender pearl-colored flesh.*

when you use them.

Peel and chop the onions and carrots. Chop the celery. Heat the vegetable oil in a roasting pan and sauté the onions, carrots, and celery with the bones and trimmings. When all ingredients are seared and lightly golden brown, add the 3 large pieces of lamb, 3 crushed garlic cloves, the bouquet garni, and one-quarter of the tomatoes, diced. Salt and pepper to taste.

Pour in the wine, and add enough water to cover the ingredients. Bring to a boil, cover, and simmer for 1 hour over low heat on top of the stove or in an oven preheated to 350°F (180°C). During this time, you can begin to prepare the Niçoise Vegetable Compote (page 50).

Remove meat from the roasting pan and place in a cool area. Strain cooking liquid through a fine mesh strainer into a saucepan. Reduce liquid over moderate heat, periodically skimming off any grease on surface and around the sides until only 3 cups (750 ml) remains. Dissolve the cornstarch in a little cold water, then whisk it briskly into the boiling juices. Remove from heat as soon as it thickens.

In a food processor with the blade attachment, grind the very cold small pieces of raw lamb into a purèe with salt, pepper, and 1 large pinch nutmeg. With the processor running, slowly pour in the heavy cream in a fine stream. Once mixture is well-blended with the texture of mousse, refrigerate. Do not overblend.

Preheat the oven to 400°F (200°C). Cut the unpeeled eggplant into ¼-inch (5 mm) thick slices. Dab a baking sheet with olive oil, arrange slices in a single layer, and lightly salt. If necessary, use a second baking sheet or cook the eggplant in two batches. Bake for 10–15 minutes, until tender. Set aside in a cool area.

Place the remaining tomatoes in boiling water for a few seconds. Refresh them under cold running water, then peel. Halve the tomatoes, then squeeze them in your hands to extract the seeds. Coarsely chop the tomatoes.

Place 2 tablespoons of olive oil in a sauté pan and add the tomatoes, salt, and pepper. Cook over high heat until all the juices are rendered and have evaporated. Set aside in a cool area.

**Several hours before serving:** Lightly oil 10 ramekins, 3 inches (8 cm) in diameter, 1½–2 inches (4–5 cm) tall. The timbales are now ready to be assembled. Set up all the cooled, prepared items near the ramekins. Line the bottom and sides of the ramekins with eggplant slices. Spread a thin layer of lamb filling in each. Cut the lamb meat into ¼-inch (5 mm) thick slices (slightly narrower than the mold). Place a lamb slice in each ramekin bottom. Cover with a layer of chopped tomatoes, then a layer of eggplant. Spread a thin layer of filling, cover with a slice of lamb, and finish by distributing the remaining mousse among the ramekins. Place the ramekins in the refrigerator.

*Cherry tomatoes stuck with a bay leaf add a great feeling of freshness.*

**30 minutes before serving:** Preheat the oven to 350°F (180°C). Arrange the ramekins in a baking pan and place in the oven. Pour in enough hot water to come almost to the rim of the pan or halfway up the sides of the molds. Cook for 30 minutes. Reheat the sauce over a low flame.

**Just before serving:** Turn the ramekins over onto separate plates and lift each ramekin straight up to release the timbale. Nap the timbales with sauce. Top each timbale with a cherry tomato stuck with a bay leaf.

**Improvise!** Add several leaves of chopped basil or a touch of garlic to sauce right after it's prepared. Remember, if there are fewer than 10 at the table, prepare all 10 ramekins anyway. Cover extras with plastic film and refrigerate for the next day.

**Wine suggestions:** Try a full-bodied red wine, such as a Châteauneuf-du-Pape or a Côte-Rôtie. Serve it just slightly cooler than *chambré* (room temperature), 57–59°F (14–15°C).

# La compote niçoise
## (Niçoise Vegetable Compote)

~

Preparation: 30 minutes
Cooking: 1 hour

Ease: Easy
Cost: Economical
Yield: 6 servings

Ingredients:
4 eggplant
3 medium zucchini
1 large onion
scant ½ cup (100 ml)
olive oil
1 red pepper
3 garlic cloves
12 basil leaves
Salt and pepper, to taste
2 tablespoons thyme flowers

**The day ahead or several hours in advance:** Peel the egg-plants with a vegetable peeler. Peel the zucchini lengthwise in alternating strips. Cut the eggplant and zucchini into ⅛-inch (2 mm) thick slices, cutting slightly on the bias. Peel the onion, chop it finely. Place 3 tablespoons of olive oil in a saucepan, add the onion, and cook gently over low heat until tender. Preheat the oven to 475°F (250°C).

Halve the red pepper, seed it, and cut it into thin strips. Place the red pepper in the pan with the onion and cook for 20 minutes over low heat. Stir the onion and red pepper together and spread them on the bottom of a baking dish in an even lay-er. Cover with a layer of eggplant. Cover the eggplant with a layer of zucchini. Repeat this step, alternating layers of egg-plant and zucchini, until the platter is full or the vegetables are used up.

Peel and chop the garlic, chop the basil. Combine them in

*Perfectly fresh from the market, a basket of ingredients for the recipes from the menu* Un déjeuner sous la tonnelle *(A Luncheon Under the Arbor).*

a bowl and stir in the remaining olive oil. Add salt and pepper according to taste. Stir in the thyme flowers. Scatter this mixture evenly over the vegetables.

Place the baking dish in the oven for 15–20 minutes. Lower the oven temperature to 325°F (160°C). Press on the vegetables with the back of a spoon so the juices rise to the surface. Continue cooking for 40–45 minutes. The vegetables are done when lightly browned, well stewed, and all the liquid released from the vegetables has evaporated.

*This dish can be served immediately after baking, or, if you have prepared it the day ahead, store it in the refrigerator.

**20 minutes before serving:** Reheat the compote in a moderate oven. Serve with Lamb and Eggplant Timbales (page 47).

# Les crêpes au miel
## et aux pignons de Provence
(Crêpes in Honey with Provençal Pine Nuts)

~

**Shopping:** *I prefer a creamy lavender or rosemary honey. If you use a nonstick pan, only half the butter is needed: 2 tablespoons (30 g) instead of 4 tablespoons (60 g).

**Several hours in advance:** Prepare the crêpe batter. Heat 2 tablespoons (30 g) of the butter in a pan over moderate heat until it turns a deep golden brown. This is called *beurre noisette*, or hazelnut butter, due to the color and nutlike smell.

With an electric mixer or whisk, combine the flour, eggs, sugar, and salt. Slowly pour in the milk and hazelnut butter in a fine stream, a bit at a time, constantly whisking. Continue to stir until a smooth batter is obtained. Pour the batter through a fine mesh strainer into a bowl. Set the batter aside to rest for at least 30 minutes.

Prepare the glaze. Warm the honey over very low heat just long enough for it to liquify, do not allow it to boil.

Preparation: 25 minutes
Cooking : 20 minutes

Ease: Fairly easy
Cost: Moderate
Yield: 6 servings

Ingredients:
*For the crêpes:*
4 tablespoons (60 g) butter
⅔ cup (90 g) sifted flour
2 large eggs
1 tablespoon plus 2
teaspoons (25 g) sugar

*(Continued on page 53)*

Immediately remove from heat.

Put well-chilled heavy cream into a tall and slightly straight sided bowl. Place the bowl of cream in a larger bowl half-full with water and ice cubes. Whip the chilled cream until it reaches firm peaks and is well aerated (be careful not to overwhip). By hand, fold the cream from the bottom upward with a whisk while gradually incorporating the egg yolks, cooled but still liquid honey, and *pastis*. Refrigerate the mixture. Lightly roast the pine nuts in a dry, ungreased pan over moderate heat, stirring the nuts often for even browning.

**20 minutes before serving:** Place 2 small crêpe pans or other skillets about 6 inches (15 cm) in diameter over moderate heat. Dab them with butter, unless they are nonstick. Pour a small ladle of well-stirred batter into the center of the pan, quickly lift the pan, and move it in circular motion until the batter evenly coats the entire surface. Cook the crêpes 1–2 minutes on each side, turning them with a metal spatula. Prepare 12 crêpes in this way.

Spread a layer of the glaze on an attractive serving platter. Fold the crêpes into quarters, and arrange them, slightly overlapping the sauce. Drizzle remaining glaze over the crêpes and sprinkle with pine nuts. Place platter under broiler for 1–2 minutes, just to lightly brown the surface.

**Improvise!** Replace the pine nuts with sliced or chopped almonds.

**Wine suggestion:** Try an aged Banyuls chilled to 54–56°F (12–13°C). Its candied fruit and spice fragrance marries well with this dessert.

1 pinch salt

6¾ fl oz (200 ml) milk

*For the glaze and garnish:*

3½ oz (100 g) flower honey *

1 cup (250 ml) heavy cream, well chilled

4 egg yolks

Several drops *pastis* (anise liquor)

*The honey harvest, richly perfumed by the garrigue.*

*Opposite: If I had invented this dessert in time, I would have wished to share it with the writer Jean Giono; through it, he would have rediscovered the fragrances of his land.*

# TUTTI FRUTTI

~

*La petite soupe de melon glacée aux fraises des bois*
*(Chilled Melon Soup with Wild Strawberries)*

*La fricassée de poulet aux figues fraîches*
*(Chicken Fricassee with Fresh Figs in Port Sauce)*

*La terrine de fruits à la crème d'amandes*
*(Assorted Fruit and Almond Cream Terrine)*

~

*A meal based on fruits served amid flowers. I wrote the menu out for the guests on a piece of cardboard cut into the shape of a pear.*

Have you ever bitten into a freshly picked plump red pepper? Sunk your teeth into a perfectly vine-ripened tomato still warm from the sun? Sensing the melting pulp and juices drip down your throat makes it easy to see that such vegetables—sweet, crisp, and fragrant—can equal the best ripe fruits.

All fruits and vegetables, before being presented as siblings on the farmers' fruit stands, originate from the same soil and are colored by the same rays of sunshine. All are the source for la *cuisine-vérité* (honest cooking), which gets its strength from the quality of the ingredients.

This enables us to understand that, as with vegetables, particular fruits marry well with particular savory dishes. All that is necessary is to establish the proper quantities, harmonizing the ingredients, and finding the right balance. The following recipes illustrate this verity. Naturally, I have chosen to use fruits that originate from Provençal soil.

*The ultra-fresh fragrances in this cocktail (recipe at right) prepares the palate, in refined elegance, to better take advantage of the menu to follow (following page).*

**For the apéritif:** Use fruits in the cocktail! This can be done very quickly. Pour a bottle of well-chilled white wine (Mâcon, Sancerre) into an attractive pitcher. Crush 3½ oz (100 g) raspberries through a fine mesh strainer. Put the pulp in the wine with 2 tablespoons cognac and 4 tablespoons *crème de framboise* (raspberry liqueur). Put a few mint leaves and several whole raspberries in iced glasses. Pour in the chilled cocktail.

# La petite soupe de melon glacée aux fraises des bois
## (Chilled Melon Soup with Wild Strawberries)

~

**Shopping:** *Choose melons with a rough, wrinkled skin, preferably *Charente* or cantaloupe for their delicate honey fragrance. A good melon should yield slightly when the end opposite the stem is gently pressed. Do not avoid melons split near the stem end; they are more likely to be especially sweet and juicy.

**At least 1½ hours before serving:** Place 6 small bowls in the refrigerator.

Cut the melons in half and scrape out the seeds with a spoon. Scoop out the flesh with a melon baller. Place the melon balls in a bowl, cover with plastic film, and refrigerate.

Collect any bits of melon that remain in the halves. Purée in a food processor with the wine, sugar, and pepper to obtain a syrup. Transfer the syrup to a bowl, cover, and refrigerate.

**1 hour before serving:** Hull the wild strawberries but, above all, do not wash them or they will be reduced to a compote and lose their fragrance.

Fill the 6 small chilled bowls with the melon balls and nap with the syrup. Divide the strawberries (or raspberries) on top. Return the bowls to the refrigerator.

**Just before serving:** Place the bowls on plates with a layer of crushed ice or decorated with a doily or strawberry leaves. Place a sprig of very fresh mint in the center of each bowl. Serve immediately.

**Improvise!** This recipe makes an attractive first course. The cantaloupe or *Charente* melon can be replaced with honeydew or even watermelon, on the condition that the strawberries or raspberries are especially flavorful.

Preparation : 25 minutes
Cooking : None

Ease: Easy
Cost: Moderate
Yield: 6 servings

Ingredients:
2 ripe melons, * 21–25 oz. (600–700 g) each
7 fl oz (200 ml) dry white wine
⅓ cup (50 g) superfine or granulated sugar
½ teaspoon freshly ground pepper
10 ½ oz. (300 g) wild strawberries or raspberries
6 small sprigs fresh mint

*Another way to present the melon soup is to use a shallow soup bowl.*

# La fricassée de poulet aux figues fraîches
## (Chicken Fricassee with Fresh Figs in Port Sauce)
~

Preparation: 40 minutes

Cooking: 1 hour

Ease: Moderate

Cost: Moderate

Yield: 6 servings

Ingredients:

12 very ripe black figs

10 fl oz (300 ml) red port

3 bay leaves

3 garlic cloves

1 large ripe tomato

3 tablespoons chopped
shallots

2 chickens, 3⅓ lbs
(1.5 kg) each

14 tablespoons (200 g) butter

Salt and pepper, to taste

2 teaspoons ground coriander

1 celery stalk

1½ teaspoons powdered
chicken bouillon †

7 oz (200 g) rice ‡

*Most amateur garden-*
*ers grow their own figs*
*in our region. If pre-*
*ferred, you can even*
*wait a bit and pick*
*them after they have*
*dried on the tree.*

**Shopping:** Ask your butcher to cut the chickens in 6 parts: 2 wings, 2 thighs, 2 drumsticks. Then request the wing tips, necks, and carcasses to be included.

†The powdered chicken bouillon (which can be replaced with 2 bouillon cubes) can be found in supermarkets or specialty stores.

‡Use long grain rice, preferably perfumed, such as basmati.

**24 hours in advance:** Place the figs in a jar with the port and 1 bay leaf. Cover and set aside to marinate.

**Several hours in advance:** Crush the garlic cloves and remove the germ. Halve the tomato and squeeze to extract the seeds. Cut the flesh in cubes. Set aside the cubed tomato, garlic, and chopped shallots (but do not combine).

Chop the chicken wing tips, necks, and carcasses.

Melt 3½ tablespoons (50 g) of the butter over moderate heat in an iron casserole. Salt and pepper the chicken pieces. Lightly brown them on all sides in the casserole. Set them aside on a plate in a warm area.

Put the all the chicken pieces in the casserole. Sear them, stirring so they brown evenly. Add the shallots and stir. Cover the casserole setting the lid slightly ajar and pour off the fat into the container.

Add the coriander, 2 bay leaves, garlic, celery, and tomato to the casserole. Pour in half of the port from the marinating figs. Arrange the chicken sections on top of the other ingredients so that they are not swimming in the cooking liquids. Cover and simmer over low heat.

Meanwhile, bring the remaining port used to marinate the figs to a boil and cook and reduce until the syrup thickens slightly. Set the syrup aside.

*This dish is all at once surprising, economical, and delicious.*

Remove the chicken pieces from the casserole. Arrange on a plate or in a bowl, cover, and set aside in a warm area. Add 5 fl oz (150 ml) water and the powdered chicken bouillon to the casserole. Cook for 10 minutes at a simmer, occasionally scraping the bottom of the pot with a wooden spoon or spatula. Pour the cooking liquid through a fine mesh strainer into a small saucepan. You should have about 5 fl oz (150 ml) of sauce.

**25 minutes before serving:** Cook the rice in salted water, following the cooking time given on the package.

Reheat the sauce over very low heat; do not let it reduce.

Place the figs in the saucepan with the reduced port. Heat gently, stirring occasionally, being careful not to crush or split the figs.

Place the chicken sections on a warm plate. Add 7 tablespoons (100 g) butter to the sauce, and stir just until it comes to a boil. Immediately take the sauce off the heat and nap it over the chicken. Arrange the glazed figs around the chicken.

Stir 3½ tablespoons (50 g) butter into the rice until melted. Serve the rice on the side.

**Chef's tip:** If you are short on time, you can omit marinating the figs in advance by placing them with the port and bay leaf in a saucepan. Cook covered, very gently over low heat for 1 hour.

**Wine suggestions:** With this dish I would serve a full-bodied red wine with a fruity, spicy nose such as a Châteauneuf-du-Pape (southern Côtes-du-Rhône) or, in a more economical vein, a Fitou (Languedoc). I would also be thrilled to uncork a Burgundy Côte de Nuits. All of these wines can be aged several years. They are all served at 57–59°F (14–15°C).

# La terrine de fruits
## à la crème d'amandes
### (Assorted Fruit and Almond Cream Terrine)

~

**Shopping:** It is usually necessary to purchase the fruits in greater quantities than needed for the recipe. Choose the best quality available, and pick out the best for the terrine.

*Pistachios are almost always sold salted. If you must buy them salted, shell and rinse them in a colander under cold water, then dry. Coarsely chop them in a food processor fitted with a blade attachment or chop with a chef's knife.

**The day ahead:** Peel the kiwi and pear. Cut the pear in large dice, then quarter and slice the kiwi. Peel the orange (see note page 36), cut it into quarters and remove the seeds if needed. Place the fruit on a paper towel, occasionally changing the towel to absorb the liquid as it is rendered.

Prepare the almond cream. Cream the butter. Add 1 cup (200 g) sugar and cream together until the mixture is light and fluffy. Incorporate the almond powder, then beat in the eggs one at a time. Whip for a fairly long time on an electric mixer or with an electric beater until the mixture is creamy, smooth, and stiff.

With a spatula, coat the bottom and sides of a 6 inch (15 cm) long cake mold with a thin, even layer of almond cream.

Arrange all the fruit (except for the strawberries) in the mold, alternating layers and types of fruit with thin layers of almond cream. Scatter chopped pistachios and candied orange peel between the layers. Finish with a layer of almond cream. Refrigerate for at least 3 hours.

Prepare a strawberry coulis. Wash and hull the strawberries and purée them in a food processor with the remaining $^1/_4$ cup (50 g) sugar. Cover and refrigerate the coulis.

**Just before serving:** Nap the bottom of 6 dessert plates with the strawberry coulis. Unmold the terrine onto a platter. Heat

Preparation: 30 minutes
Cooking: None

Ease: Easy
Cost: Moderate
Yield: 6 servings

Ingredients:
3 oz (90 g) kiwi
3 oz (90 g) pear
1$^1/_2$ oranges
2$^1/_2$ sticks (300 g) butter, softened
1$^1/_4$ cup (250 g) sugar
7$^1/_2$ oz (210 g) almond powder
3 eggs
1$^3/_4$ oz (50 g) white grapes
1$^3/_4$ oz (50 g) black grapes
1 tablespoon pistachios, * coarsely chopped
1 tablespoon candied orange peel
9 oz (250 g) strawberries

a long bladed knife under hot water and cut 6 slices, placing each on top of the coulis on the plates.

**Chef's tips:** The following will make it easier to unmold the terrine: Before spreading on the first layer of almond cream, line the entire terrine with plastic film so that it extends over the rim of the terrine. When the terrine is ready to be unmolded, place a platter over the terrine, and turn both the platter and terrine over. Lift the mold straight up off the terrine and remove the plastic film.

To facilitate cutting the slices, place a cake knife or large metal spatula at the end of the terrine, holding the end in place while cutting the slice with a hot knife. Catch the slice on the cake knife or spatula and transfer it to a plate.

This terrine can be prepared the day ahead, but do not keep it for more than 36 hours or the fruit will start to break down and release its juices.

*The soft green shell that houses the almond reveals the delicate, yet at the same time strong, flavor of the fresh nut inside.*

**Wine suggestion:** This is the moment to sample a Muscat appellation Beaumes-de Venise (southern Côtes-du-Rhône), a natural, soft, extraordinary fruity wine. Chill it to 50°F (10°C).

*Other fruits can be used in this terrine, including blackberries, figs, plums, red currants, and peaches. They all allow you to re-invent the terrine according to the market's inspiration.*

# UN AIR DE VACANCES
## (IN THE HOLIDAY MOOD)

~

*Le gaspacho de thon et saumon frais*
*(Fresh Tuna and Salmon Gazpacho)*

*La salade d'écrevisses en sauce crème*
*(Crayfish Salad with Cream Sauce)*

*Le cocktail de fruits rouges au champagne*
*(Red Fruit Cocktail with Champagne)*

~

Vacations are parentheses during which we leave a cozy, snug abode for another, often less comfortable, but perhaps situated closer to a dream several hundred miles away. We abandon obligations, proprieties, and habits for rediscovery—but what that is depends on you.

*Under the morning sun, the fisherman returns to port in Cassis; there will be fresh fish for lunch.*

Some rediscover other obligations, proprieties, and habits, and sometimes even their next-door neighbors. Others, like myself, profit to rediscover their childhood. Along with your winter clothes, pack up your dignity and seriousness in the mothballs. Rediscover the sentiments you've set aside in the past and learn how it feels to move freely. After all, it was only yesterday. Give your senses carte blanche to openly rediscover real luxury; treat yourself to delicious, exquisite meals, relaxed as when wearing a favorite old polo shirt.

Casually crumble your bread in the gazpacho, eat your dessert in a glass filled with champagne bubbles. You wouldn't do this at home during a chic dinner? Exactly, that is what I mean by vacations!

**For the apéritif:** Since you have already opened a bottle of champagne to prepare the dessert, serve the rest before sitting at the table, although it may mean rounding off the apéritif by popping open a second cork!

# Le gaspacho de thon et saumon frais
## (Fresh Tuna and Salmon Gazpacho)

~

Preparation: 35 minutes

Cooking: None

Ease: Easy

Cost: Moderate

Yield: 6 servings

Ingredients:

2 ¾ lbs (1.2 kg) very

ripe tomatoes *

1 cucumber

1 red bell pepper

1 garlic clove

Salt, to taste

4 tablespoons olive oil

2 tablespoons wine vinegar

Tabasco

1 medium new white onion

1 tablespoon parsley, finely

chopped

1 tablespoon tarragon, finely

chopped

5 oz (150 g) tuna filet †

5 oz (150 g) salmon filet †

Juice of ½ lemon

*Garlic, tarragon, and olive oil mingle with the other fragrances in this recreated gazpacho. It's also easy to imagine this soup garnished with chives.*

**Shopping:** *For the tomatoes, I prefer plum tomatoes for this gazpacho. They are small, oblong, and are best found at the height of the season.

†The tuna and salmon should be as absolutely fresh as possible. If unavailable, any other very fresh saltwater fish can be substituted. For the tuna, ask for a section from the belly of a large white tuna; the tail meat has tough nerves. Insist on fresh salmon that has never been frozen, preferably Scottish or Norwegian.

**2 or 3 hours in advance:** Halve the tomatoes and press them gently in your hand to extract the juices and seeds. Peel the cucumber, halve lengthwise, and scrape out the seeds with a small spoon. Cut off the red-pepper stem, halve the pepper, and seed it. Set half aside. Peel the garlic and set half aside

In a food processor, purée the tomatoes, garlic, and the half amounts of cucumber and red pepper. Salt to taste, and add the olive oil, vinegar, and 2–3 drops of tabasco. Taste the soup to check the seasoning. Pour the soup through a fine mesh strainer; after straining it should have the consistency of light cream.

Peel the onion and chop it finely; then put it in a fine mesh strainer and rinse it under cold water. Cut the remaining cucumber and red pepper in very small dice, the same size as the onion. Stir the parsley and tarragon into the diced vegetables. Refrigerate the mixture.

**15 minutes before serving:** Place a large plate in the refrigerator. Clean the fish fillets, removing any skin and bones. Rinse and dry them. Cut the fillets into slices 1½–2 inches (4–5 cm) long and ⅛-inch (3 mm) thick. Place the slices on the chilled plate. Salt lightly, and sprinkle with the lemon juice. Refrigerate so the fish can marinate for 10 minutes, *no more!*

**Just before serving:** Divide the slices of fish among 6 shallow soup bowls, nap with the puréed vegetables and sprinkle the small dice of vegetables and herbs on top. Serve immediately.

**Improvise!** Sometimes I replace the fish with shelled shrimp and scallops, provided they are very fresh.

**Wine suggestion:** Uncork a dry white wine such as a cassis, chilled to 46–48°F (8–9°C) in an ice bucket with ice cubes and cold water.

## La salade d'écrevisses en sauce crème
### (Crayfish Salad with Cream Sauce)

~

**Shopping:** Crayfish, lobsterettes (*langoustines*), and large shrimp are best ordered in advance so that you can insist on their being alive upon purchase. A crustacean releases its waste soon after it dies, rendering it unsuitable for consumption. If you have the good luck to find wild crayfish, remove the intestines just before cooking them. To do this, hold the head in one hand, and with the thumb and index finger of the other hand take hold of the center flipper at the top of the tail and quickly pull backward, giving a quarter turn to remove the black shaft of intestines at the same time. This step is less important for the farm-raised crayfish commonly purchased in fish stores; generally, they have not eaten for 2 or 3 days so the intestines are empty.

Preparation: 30 minutes
Cooking: 15 minutes

Ease: Moderate
Cost: Expensive
Yield: 6 servings

*(Continued on page 69)*

**3 or 4 hours in advance:** Peel the cucumbers and slice them thinly. Sprinkle the slices with 2 teaspoons fine salt and set aside to degorge. When their water has been rendered, rinse them with cold water and drain well.

In a casserole, heat 1½ gallons (6 liters) water with 3 tablespoons coarse salt and the bouquet garni. At first boil, add the crayfish. Boil for 2 minutes. Turn off the heat and set aside for the crayfish to cool in the cooking liquid.

Meanwhile, prepare the *nage*. Very finely slice the carrots, onion, celery, and shallots. In a saucepan, heat 8 tablespoons of water, the white wine, salt, and pepper. At first boil, add the vegetables. When the water comes back to a boil, lower the heat and simmer for 2 minutes. After cooling, store the bouillon and vegetables in the refrigerator.

**20 minutes before serving:** Combine the chilled bouillon and vegetables with the yogurt and crème fraîche (or cream); add salt and pepper to taste.

Shell the crayfish, set aside 6 heads for the presentation. Combine the crayfish tails, cucumbers, dill, chervil, and the sauce. Check the seasoning, adding salt and pepper if needed. Divide the salad among six chilled bowls. Sprinkle with chopped egg and decorate each serving with a crayfish head.

**Improvise!** I sometimes replace the dill with the same quantity of chopped tarragon.

**Wine suggestions:** You may continue with the same cassis served with the gazpacho, or uncork a dry white Bordeaux, a Graves appellation. In either case, serve at 46–50°F (8–10°C).

*Once prepared, the crayfish salad should be kept chilled in the refrigerator; and don't hold the dessert for longer than a few minutes after you've prepared it.*

2 medium cucumbers

coarse salt

1 bouquet garni:

3–4 sprigs parsley, 1 bay leaf, 2 sprigs thyme, 1 large bunch dill or tarragon, tied together

4½–5½ lbs (2–2.5 kg) crayfish or 4½ lbs (2 kg) lobsterettes (*langoustines*) or large shrimp

1 carrot

1 small onion

¾ oz (20 g) celery

¾ oz (20 g) shallots

8 tablespoons dry white wine

Salt and pepper, to taste

4½ oz (125 g) yogurt, well chilled

1 tablespoon crème fraîche (or heavy cream), well chilled

1 tablespoon coarsely chopped dill

1 tablespoon coarsely chopped chervil

1 hard-boiled egg, chopped

*Artists in harmony: the Cocktail de fruits rouges au champagne (Red Fruit Cocktail with Champagne) set before a canvas signed by artist Charles Atamian (following double page).*

# Le cocktail de fruits rouges au champagne
## (Red Fruit Cocktail with Champagne)

~

Preparation: 30 minutes

Cooking: 5 minutes

Ease: Easy

Cost: Expensive

Yield: 6 servings

Ingredients:

½ pint (200 g) strawberries

½ pint (200 g) wild strawberries

½ pint (200 g) raspberries

½ pint (200 g) red currants

¾ cup (170 g) sugar

½ bottle champagne, well chilled

**Several hours in advance:** Wash the strawberries in a strainer under cold water, dry and hull them. Do not wash the wild strawberries (they are too fragile and become mushy), or the raspberries (they absorb too much water and lose their flavor). Place each fruit on a separate plate.

Wash the red currants, dry them, and pick them off the stems. Set half aside on a plate. In a small saucepan, heat the other half of the red currants with 2 tablespoons water and ⅓ cup (70 g) sugar. At the first boil, remove pan from heat and set aside to cool. Transfer the currants to a bowl lined with a few layers of cheesecloth. Lift up the edges of the cheesecloth and gather the sides together to form a pouch, then turn the pouch to squeeze out the juice from the currants into the bowl.

Place the remaining sugar on a plate. Dip the rims of 6 glasses into the red-currant syrup, shake off any excess syrup, then set the moistened rims in the sugar to adhere and decorate.

Being careful not to touch the sugared rims, fill the glasses two-thirds full with the assorted fruit. Divide the red-currant syrup among the glasses, pouring it over the fruit.

**Just before serving:** Place the glasses on small dessert plates. Bring the glasses to the table. At this moment, and not before, fill the glasses with champagne to ½ inch (1 cm) from the rim. A beautiful pink foam from the champagne and berries will rise to crown the glasses.

*Always wash and dry red currants before picking them off their stems, never the reverse, or they will lose their juices and fragrance.*

**Improvise!** All the fruits can be interchanged with black currants, blueberries, or other fruits of choice. You can even use only one type of fruit, except for the red currants which, by themselves, would make the cocktail too acidic. On the other hand, if you completely omit the red currants the cocktail will be too sweet, in which case you can make up for the lost acidity with the juice of half a lemon.

**Presentation suggestion:** With scissors, cut from the edge to the center of 6 small paper doilies. Place the doilies around the foot of each glass and slip a small flower into each slit.

# UN DÉJEUNER DE FLEURS

## (A LUNCHEON OF FLOWERS)

~

*Les fleurs de courgettes farcies aux champignons*
*(Stuffed Zucchini Flowers with Truffles)*

*Le carré d'agneau rôti à la fleur de thym*
*(Roast Rack of Lamb with Thyme Flowers)*

*Les tartelettes d'orange meringuées, fleurs de lavande*
*(Orange Meringue Tartlets with Lavender Flowers)*

~

*Flowers on the table and all around; they make the best decoration for a menu in which they are presented on the plate as well.*

When I lived in Var (a county in the Provence region), I lived on a farm where we cultivated vegetables, flowers, and grape vines. Having been away for several weeks, I returned one moonless night. A little hungry, I steered myself in the dark toward what I remembered to be a patch of mesclun salad. I picked several leaves that impressed me as being quite tender. After seasoning it with a touch of garlic, I very much appreciated this new and pleasant-tasting salad.

But the next morning my friend Félix, a farmer, grumbled, "I don't know who destroyed my marigold seedlings. Look at this massacre!" I laughed, confessing that I was the guilty one, deceived by the moon.

Félix poked fun at me, declaring that in Provence we were used to eating quite a few types of plants and flowers in salads, but marigolds—no one was ever crazy enough to try. You really have to be a Parisian to swallow those (For him, "Parisian" designated all individuals coming from north of Aix in Provence). Regardless of my "foreign" origins, I was finally adopted after making innumerable toasts around *pastis*. Down there, in Saint-Clair, one was quickly accepted if one loved *pastis*, jokes, and *pétanque*. My, how sweet life was, warmed by friendship and lacking in difficulties. Except when it came to salads!

Another familiar rich vegetation from Provence is thyme. The best thyme comes from the *garrigue* and cannot be found below 650 feet (200 meters) in elevation—a few bird flights from the sea. It only grows on the rocky slopes burned by the sun, where it is submitted to assaults by the *mistral* (the famed Provençal wind) and grazing sheep. It rarely grows more than 6 inches (15 cm) tall. Drenched by the last of the winter rains that revive the sparse hills in the pretty month of May, this thyme is dressed in blue-pink flowers that watercolor the Provençal hills and gently awaken the bee hives. Their splendor lasts only two weeks.

The wild flowers in this menu (no marigolds!) keep you away from the table for several moments between serving each course. Take on this small constraint as a real chef; that is to say, by thinking first of the happiness of your guests. I do not know any better example than my late friend Danny Kaye. This great actor (who was also a great cook) never sat down before having served each person himself. His happiness was derived from the pleasure he could give. Bravo, chef!

**For the apéritif:** Stick with flowers, without exaggerating. But do not make drinks based on the sole pretext of fragrance, as did the restaurateur who served Paul Bocuse and me a lemon sorbet "Chanel no. 5." After this even an aïoli was eaten without recognition! Rather, simply blend 5 tablespoons Cointreau with one 25 fl oz (750 ml) of champagne. Serve it quickly before the bubbles start to fade, adding ½ teaspoon of orange-flower water to each glass.

*These highly decorative nasturtium flowers brighten up any dishes you wish to animate with strong color. Moreover, they release a delicious piquant, peppery flavor.*

# Les fleurs de courgettes farcies
## aux champignons
### (Stuffed Zucchini Flowers with Truffles)

~

**Shopping:** *Zucchini flowers are becoming easier to find at farmers' markets. To be safe, order them ahead. They are usually attached to small zucchini (if not, they are probably squash flowers). They wilt quickly, but will last longer if you store them in a bowl of cold water. You can replace them with pumpkin flowers (remove the pistils), boiled Swiss chard leaves, or even boiled tender green cabbage leaves.
†The most tender spinach leaves are the small new leaves that sprout in springtime. If unavailable, choose the small and light-colored center leaves, or replace them with *mâche* (lamb's quarters). Cut the stems and use only the leaves; even after washing, there is often some sand that clings near the roots.

**Several hours in advance:** Cut the sandy bottoms off the mushroom stems. Wash the mushrooms in a colander under the faucet and dry well. Chop them in large dice. Put them in a bowl and stir in the lemon juice.

Heat 2 tablespoons (30 g) of the butter and the shallots in a sauté pan. As soon as you hear and see the butter bubble, add the mushrooms and salt, stir and cook for 3-4 minutes.

Drain the mushrooms in a fine mesh strainer over a small saucepan. Set the cooking liquid aside for later use. Return the mushrooms to the sauté pan and dry them out over high heat, stirring constantly. Remove from heat.

In a bowl, whisk the heavy cream and egg yolks together. Season with salt and pepper, then add the mixture to the mushrooms. Cook for 2 minutes, stirring briskly. Set aside to cool on a large plate. Drain, adding the cooking liquid to the small saucepan with the mushroom liquid.

Gently wipe the zucchini flowers if necessary. Place 1 teaspoon mushroom purée inside the center of each flower. Close

Preparation: 25 minutes
Cooking: 25 minutes

Ease: Easy
Cost: Inexpensive (though truffle variations may be very expensive)
Yield: 6 servings

Ingredients:
1 lb (500 g) white mushrooms
Juice of ½ lemon
2 ½ sticks (280 g) butter
1 tablespoon chopped shallot
Salt and pepper, to taste
5 tablespoons heavy cream
2 egg yolks
6 zucchini flowers *
7 oz (200 g) young, tender spinach or *mâche* †
1 large bunch fresh rosemary chervil sprigs

the petals. Place the well-sealed flowers in a steaming basket (such as one used for vegetables or couscous) and cover with a sheet of aluminum foil.

Stem, wash, and drain the spinach.

Bring the mushroom cooking liquid to a boil and reduce until only 3 tablespoons remain. Cut the remaining butter into small pieces. Briskly whisk the pieces in batches, into the mushroom liquid over high heat. Add a pinch of salt and pepper, then set the sauce aside.

**20 minutes before serving:** Fill the bottom of a steamer pot with hot water and add the rosemary. Bring to a boil over high heat. Put the zucchini flowers into the steamer basket and place over the boiling water. Cover and cook for 15 minutes. To check for doneness, the tip of a knife should be able to pierce the zucchini flower without any resistance.

Meanwhile, reheat the sauce in a hot water bath or double boiler.

**Just before serving:** Arrange the raw spinach leaves or *mâche* on 6 hot plates. Place the stuffed, steamed zucchini flowers on top, salt lightly, and give one turn of the pepper mill. Nap the flowers with the mushroom butter.

**Decoration suggestion:** Scatter several chervil sprigs over the finished plates and serve immediately.

**My elegant variation:** This delicate dish becomes grandiose with the addition of truffles. Use 6 canned Vaucluse black truffles 1/2 oz (15 g). (Try to find truffles marked *de première cuisson,* or first cooking.) Place them whole in the egg-cream-mushroom mixture when it is set aside to cool. Reserve the liquid from the truffle can and reduce it with the mushroom liquid. Continue, following the same above procedure for preparing the mushroom stuffing.

*Zucchini flowers only stay fresh for the one day on which they bloom. Purchase them no sooner than the morning of the same day they are to be prepared.*

If with any luck you are able to obtain fresh truffles, place them in a small hermetically sealed jar and wrap the jar in a kitchen towel. Place the jar in a saucepan filled with boiling water, cover, and cook for 30 minutes. Proceed with the recipe in the same way as indicated for the canned truffles.

**Wine suggestion:** Try a dry white wine from the northern Côtes-du-Rhône, such as a Condrieu, chosen young for its iris and violet fragrance. Serve chilled 46–50°F (8–10°C).

# Le carré d'agneau rôti à la fleur de thym
## (Roast Rack of Lamb with Thyme Flowers)
~

**Shopping:** *The racks of lamb merit being ordered in advance. This will give your butcher the chance to procure a good quality lamb and to prepare the racks from the first 9 chops and French them (trim the meat and fat between the top third of each rib). Ask the butcher to give you the trimmings and bone on the side.
†Young garlic harvested at the end of spring is ideal for this recipe; it does not contain the green germ that grows in the older cloves and renders them less digestible.
‡If the sublime thyme flower taken from a *garrigue* (see page 76) is unavailable, use the flowers from common thyme, providing that it has grown in the sun in a poor, dry soil.

**1 hour and 15 minutes before serving:** Separate the garlic cloves, one by one, without peeling. Soak them in cold water for 15–20 minutes, then drain.

Meanwhile, preheat the oven to the highest possible temperature. Spread the trimmings and bone on the bottom of a roasting pan, removing as much fat as possible.

Score the fat side of the racks making incisions 1 inch (3 cm) apart in a criss-cross pattern, cutting as deeply as possible into the fat without cutting into the meat. Salt both sides and sprinkle with thyme flowers. Place the racks in the roasting pan with

Preparation: 15 minutes
Cooking: 25 minutes

Ease: Easy
Cost: Moderate
Yield: 6 servings

Ingredients:
2 heads garlic or 20 firm garlic cloves †
3 racks of lamb, * first cut, about 2 ½ lbs (1.2 kg) each
Salt and pepper, to taste
3 tablespoons thyme flowers ‡
1 large bunch thyme
6 tablespoons butter

*Toward the end of spring, purchase a beautiful bunch of green-stemmed garlic. Hang it in the kitchen to remind yourself to use it in all your dishes: garlic is a guarantee for good health.*

the fat side up. Do not add any fat, oil, or butter to the pan.

Roast for 10 minutes. Add the garlic cloves without turning the racks. Cook for 10 minutes more then turn the racks over so the fat side is on the bottom. Cook for 5 minutes more.

Take the racks out of the oven and place them on a small plate set upside-down on top of a large plate. Remove the garlic cloves and set aside. Cover the racks with a sheet of aluminum foil and keep them hot by placing them in the oven, turned off, with the door cracked open. This will allow the racks to release their juices without soaking in them.

Press on one end of each garlic clove to push it out of its skin. Put the peeled cloves in the oven in a covered, heatproof dish to keep them warm.

*If you serve the tartlets on individual plates, place a small bouquet of fresh lavender on the side. If you present them on a pretty platter, slide sprigs of lavender between them.*

With a spoon or bulb baster, skim off the grease that rises to the surface of the cooking juices in the roasting pan. Add 3½ fl oz (100 ml) hot water to pan and scrape to loosen drippings. Pour this mixture into a saucepan, reduce by half over high heat. Add the thyme sprigs, cover, and set aside to infuse for 10 minutes off the heat.

**Just before serving:** If necessary, reheat the racks for several minutes in the oven. Lightly brown the garlic cloves with butter in a sauté pan. Remove the thyme and pour the meat juices through a fine mesh strainer into a saucepan. As soon as the garlic cloves are golden brown, add them to the saucepan with the juices.

Cut the racks into chops. Arrange them on a hot platter or on hot plates. Season with a grind of fresh pepper, serve immediately with the sauce on the side.

**My accompaniment:** Don't try to complicate this simple dish of delicious fragrances. Your guests will be delighted with a side of small new potatoes.

**Wine suggestions:** Serve a red wine with a fresh, fruity nose such as a Volnay, Santenay (Burgundy), or a Fleurie (Beaujolais).

# Les tartelettes d'orange meringuées, fleurs de lavande
## (Orange Meringue Tartlets with Lavender Flowers)
~

The dough recipe will yield more than required, but it is easiest to prepare a larger than needed quantity. The extra amount stores well in the refrigerator or freezer.

**Shopping:** *It is easier to find dried lavender flowers than fresh lavender branches and they are also a better buy. Most importantly, do not purchase lavender flowers used to scent clothing, as they are usually perfumed with a very strong extract that

Preparation: 35 minutes
Cooking: 35 minutes

Ease: Fairly easy
Cost: Inexpensive
Yield: 6 servings

*(Continued on page 84)*

## Ingredients:

*For the dough ( 18 shells):*
1¾ cups (250 g) flour, sifted
¾ cup (150 g) sugar
1 pinch salt
14 tablespoons (200 g) butter,
softened
4 egg yolks

*For the filling (makes 6 tarts):*
1 lemon
1 orange
1 cup (200 g) sugar
4 tablespoons (60 g) butter,
softened
3 whole eggs

*For the meringue:*
3 egg whites
4 oz (120 g) confectioners'
sugar, sifted

*For the decoration:*
1 teaspoon lavender flowers *

would ruin your dessert. If you can not find fresh lavender flowers, forego them. The tartlets will still be very good.

**At least 3½ hours before the meal:** Place the tartlet molds in the refrigerator.

Prepare the dough. In a food processor fitted with the cutting blade, combine the flour, sugar, and 1 pinch salt. Add the butter and egg yolks. Process on low speed. As soon as the dough begins to come together, take it out of the machine and shape it into a ball with your hands. Wrap it in plastic film or a lightly dampened kitchen towel and refrigerate for at least 1 hour.

Prepare the filling. Wash the lemon and orange, cut into quarters, and seed. *Do not peel.* In the food processor, combine the sugar, softened butter, eggs, and orange and lemon quarters. Process until the mixture is puréed. Place the filling in the refrigerator until needed.

Roll out the dough to ⅛-inch (2 mm) thick. Cut out 6 circles of dough, 4 inches (10 cm) in diameter each. Take the tartlet molds out of the refrigerator and line them with the dough. Trim off any dough that extends over the edge of the molds, and prick the bottom of the dough with a fork. Return the lined tartlet molds to the refrigerator for at least 30 minutes.

**At least 2 hours before the meal:** Preheat the oven to 400°F (200°C). Place the lined molds on a baking sheet and bake for 10 minutes. Take them out of the oven, but leave the oven on.

Fill each tartlet shell with the orange-lemon cream. Return the filled shells to the oven and bake for 20 minutes. Turn off the oven. Set the shells aside, taking them off the baking sheet to cool for 10 minutes before unmolding. Return the unmolded tartlets to the baking sheet, but do not place them in the oven. Preheat the oven to 320°F (160°C).

Prepare the meringue. Whip the egg whites to very firm peaks. Slowly and gradually add the confectioners' sugar, whipping constantly until you obtain a thick, shiny meringue. Dollop 1 tablespoon of meringue on each tartlet, spreading it

to form a dome with a spatula. Sprinkle the lavender flowers on top.

**30 minutes before serving:** Heat the tartlets for 5 minutes in the oven. Present them slightly warmed on dessert plates.

**Chef's tip:** For a dough of even thickness, cut 2 narrow strips of wood 20-inches (50 cm) long and ⅛-inch thick. (You can vary thicknesses for other recipe needs.) To use, place one set strips on either side of the dough. Press the rolling pin over them and roll the dough until the wood strips and dough sheet are at equal heights.

*To perfectly whip egg whites, bring eggs to room temperature 1 hour in advance. Use a clean, dry bowl completely free of any fat or egg traces and add a pinch of fine salt before whipping. When you can spin the bowl a full turn and the whites stay in place without falling from the sides, they are ready.

*Here is the secret for poppy liqueur, a logical finish to a luncheon based on flowers: Making sure they are free of any dew, crush stemmed poppy flowers. Seal them in an airtight jar with an equal volume of unflavored eau-de-vie and the zest of 1 lemon. Set aside in a cool dark place for 10 days. Strain the liquid. Prepare a syrup based on an equal volume of sugar and water, totaling half of the volume of the infusion. Bring the sugar and water to a boil, then set aside to cool. Stir the cooled syrup into the infusion—and it's ready!*

# MENU DE FÊTE
## (A PARTY MENU)

~

*La coquille de brouillade d'œufs au caviar*
*(Scrambled Eggs in their Shells with Caviar)*

*La fricassée de homard à la crème d'estragon*
*(Lobster Fricassee with Tarragon Cream Sauce)*

*Les filets d'agneau en croûte et duxelles de cèpes*
*(Lamb Fillets in Puff Pastry with Duxelle of Wild Mushrooms)*

*Le soufflé glacé aux fraises*
*(Frozen Strawberry Soufflés)*

~

*Along with the mouillettes (finger toasts), don't forget to place a small coffee spoon at each place setting.*

You will not need to improvise on this grandiose and refined celebratory menu. Yet, it will respond according to the season at the market, and, it is possible to imagine, the luck you encounter shopping in specialty stores. This is similar to the way I prepare meals each year during my stays in Los Angeles. I always take the opportunity to invite several actor friends (often more than thirty), such as Sharon Stone, Michael Douglas, Lee Marvin, Jack Nicholson, Anthony Quinn, Sylvester Stallone, and Arnold Schwarzenegger, among others.

The excursion to the farmers' market is the kickoff for the party; this is where gourmet dreams are composed, while salivating in front of the most beautiful products. The result is often a menu based on simple dishes (such as chestnut soup, fish roasted with tomatoes and olives, and lamb stew with potatoes and vegetables). Each guest may bring appropriate bottles from their wine cellar. With the gastronomic improvisations a success, the party swells more and more magnificently, fueled by the abundance of delicious food and the happiness of shared sensations.

Under such happy circumstances, it is necessary to know how to be extravagant. Therefore, for this lavish menu I have devised four courses instead of three. Here amity rhymes with generosity.

**For the apéritif:** Before starting such a dinner, champagne is the required apéritif for everyone! Fifteen to twenty minutes before uncorking the bottle, plunge it into an ice bucket filled with cold water and floating ice cubes. The ideal serving temperature is 46–48°F (8–9°C). To begin with absolute sumptuousness, serve little toasts of country bread covered with thin slices of black truffle and sprinkled with several grains of coarse salt, a turn of the pepper mill, and several drops of very fruity olive oil.

*To serve champagne from an ice bucket without dripping water everywhere, wrap the shoulder of the bottle using a pretty white napkin as though it were a scarf.*

# La coquille de brouillade d'œufs au caviar
### (Scrambled Eggs in their Shells with Caviar)

~

**Several hours in advance:** Very carefully cut off the wider end of the top of each egg, keeping the shells intact. Empty the eggs into a bowl. Wash the shells, and set them aside to dry, turned over on a kitchen towel.

Whip the eggs with a whisk and season with salt and pepper. Pour the eggs through a fine mesh strainer to eliminate any bits of egg shell. Place the strained eggs in the refrigerator.

**10 minutes before serving:** Heat the butter in a small saucepan over low heat. Pour in the whisked eggs. Gently stir with a wooden spatula until they take on a creamy texture. Scrape against the bottom and corners of the pan to prevent the eggs from becoming lumpy. Take the pan off the heat and add the crème fraîche (or cream). Season to taste with salt and pepper. Place the eggshells in egg cups and fill the shells with the scrambled egg. Toast the bread slices and cut them into long, narrow "fingers."

Place 2 teaspoons (10 g) caviar on top of each egg; stick 4–5 chive stems into the eggs.

**Chef's tip:** The ideal way to cleanly cut off the top of the eggshells is with egg scissors (found in specialty stores).

**Variation:** Replace the bread fingers with small 2½–3 inch (7–8 cm) long asparagus tips. Boil them for 1 minute in salted water, drain, and serve hot.

**Wine suggestion:** Don't change to a different wine, just continue with the same champagne served for the apéritif!

Preparation: 30 minutes
Cooking: About 10 minutes

Ease: Easy
Cost: Expensive
Yield: 6 servings

Ingredients:
6 extra-large eggs
Salt and pepper, to taste
2 tablespoons (30 g) butter
3 teaspoons crème fraîche (or heavy cream)
3 slices white bread
2 oz (60 g) beluga or sevruga caviar
1 small bunch chives

# La fricassée de homard à la crème d'estragon

## (Lobster Fricassee with Tarragon Cream Sauce)

~

**Shopping:** *Regardless of whether you choose lobsters or rock lobsters, order them in advance to be sure to get live, good-quality crustaceans.

**Several hours in advance:** Before preparing the lobsters, it is important to know if you are a sensitive person or not. If you are, preheat the oven to 475°F (240°C). Place the lobsters on the oven rack. They will not have time to think, they will already be in gourmet heaven. Cook them for 4 minutes, then remove from the oven. Halve them lengthwise by planting the tip of a chef's knife at the joint between the head and the tail perpendicular to the lobster. Lower the knife in the direction of the tail and cut all the way through.

If you are a less sensitive person, cut the lobsters the same way as indicated above, but while they are alive. This way is faster.

Gently crush the claws with the flat side of a chef's knife being careful not to damage the meat. In 1 large or 2 medium sauté pans (whichever can best contain the 12 lobster halves when snugly placed together), very lightly brown the butter and chopped shallots over moderate heat. Arrange the lobster halves on top, cut side down, shell side up. Cook for 3 minutes.

Turn the lobsters over and cover the meat side with crème fraîche (or cream). Separate the leaves from the tarragon stems and add the stems to the sauté pan. Cover the pan as tightly as possible. Bring to a boil over a low flame, then cook for 6 minutes. Turn off the heat.

Remove the lobster halves from the pan, pouring off any crème fraîche from their shells back into pan. Remove the lobster meat from the shells in one piece, being careful not to crush the meat. Carefully remove the meat from the claws.

Preparation time: 35 minutes
Cooking: 20 minutes

Ease: Easy
Cost: Expensive
Yield: 6 servings

Ingredients:
6 lobsters,* (or rock lobsters)
about 1 lb (400 g) each
6 tablespoons (90 g) butter
3 shallots, chopped
30 fl oz (900 ml) crème
fraîche (or heavy cream)
6 stems tarragon
Salt and pepper, to taste

*Two beautiful specimens chosen for their perfect freshness. We picked a bouquet of fresh tarragon to offer them.*

*For the presentation, follow this model.*

Place all the lobster meat into a large saucepan.

Empty the contents of the lobster heads into the sauté pan the lobsters were cooked in. On a plate, set aside the empty heads with the 2 small claws still attached (the top set below the large claws). Add the empty claw shells, tail shells, and any other shells and scraps to the sauté pan. Bring to a boil, then pour the cooking liquid through a fine mesh strainer into the saucepan with the lobster meat. Add a pinch of salt.

**10 or 20 minutes before serving:** Reheat the sauce for 20 minutes over a hot water bath or double boiler, or for 10 minutes directly on low heat.

**Just before serving:** Add the chopped tarragon leaves and give 3 turns with the pepper mill to the sauce. Per serving, place 2 lobster halves and the meat from 2 claws on a hot plate. Nap generously with the sauce. Decorate with a lobster head.

**Improvise!** This recipe is also very flavorful if you replace the tarragon with 1 teaspoon of *pastis*, adding it to the sauce just before serving.

**Wine suggestion:** This is the moment to uncork a white Châteauneuf-du-Pape. Choose a sumptuous year (see wine chart, page 17) and chill to 46–48°F (8–9°C).

## Les filets d'agneau en croûte et duxelle de cèpes
### (Lamb Fillets in Puff Pastry with Duxelle of Wild Mushrooms)

Preparation: 1 hour, 30 minutes

Cooking: 1 hour

*(Continued on next page)*

**Shopping:** *The lamb fillets should be taken from a cleanly trimmed lamb saddle; that is clean of fat, skin, and bone.
†If you wish to save a bit of money, use 1 oz (30 g) dried porcini combined with ¾ lb (350 g) white mushrooms. Rehydrate the

porcini for 15 minutes in 2 cups (500 ml) warm water. Drain, squeeze out the excess water, and chop along with the white mushrooms, and continue the recipe as indicated.

**Several hours in advance:** *The puff pastry:* Use a food processor fitted with the blade attachment, or an electric stand mixer fitted with a hook attachment.

Cut the butter into small pieces. Dissolve the salt in the water. Put the butter and flour in the food processor or the bowl of the mixer and process. While blending, gradually pour in a little water at a time until the dough comes away from the sides (several seconds in the food processor, or 1-2 minutes in the mixer). Wrap the dough in plastic film and refrigerate for 20 minutes.

On a work surface dusted with flour, roll out half of the dough with a rolling pin into a rectangle 20 inches (50 cm) long by 8 inches (20 cm) wide. Refrigerate the other half of the dough for another use. Fold the ends of the rectangle of dough so they meet at the center, then fold them over on themselves (folding the dough in half) as if to close a book. Wrap in plastic film and refrigerate for 20 minutes. Place the dough in front of you so the fold is to the left. Roll out the dough into a rectangle the same size as the first, 20 inches (50 cm) by 8 inches (20 cm). Fold the rectangle the same way as the first time. Wrap the dough in plastic wrap and refrigerate for 15 minutes. Roll out the dough for a third time into a rectangle and fold it as before. Wrap it and refrigerate until needed.
*The lamb stock:* Start preparing the stock during the time the puff pastry dough is resting in the refrigerator.

Heat the olive oil in a stock pot. Lightly brown the bones. Pour off the fat into a heatproof container.

To the pot add the shallots, carrots, thyme, garlic, bay leaf, and tomato paste. Sweat the mixture over low heat. Add the wine, a few peppercorns and cook until the liquid is reduced by three-quarters.

Ease: Difficult
Cost: Expensive
Yield: 6 servings

Ingredients:
*For the puff pastry:* *
1⅓ cup (300 g) butter
2 teaspoons salt
3 cups (500 g) flour
1 cup (240 ml) cold water

*For the lamb stock:*
3 tablespoons olive oil
1 lb (450 g) lamb bones *
4 shallots, coarsely chopped
1 medium carrot, coarsely chopped
1 thyme sprig
1 small head garlic, chopped
1 bay leaf
1 teaspoon tomato paste
11 fl oz (330 ml) wine (of that which will also accompany the dish)
Several peppercorns
½ cube chicken bouillon
Salt and pepper, to taste

*For the lamb fillets:*
2 tablespoons vegetable oil
1 tablespoon butter
Salt and pepper, to taste
1 lb (500 g) lamb fillets, * cut from the saddle

(Continued on page 94)

*For the duxelles:*
¾ lb (350 g) fresh cèpes (or porcini) mushrooms †
1 tablespoon shallots, chopped
1 tablespoon butter
Salt and pepper, to taste

*For the stuffing: †*
5 oz (150 g) skinless, boneless chicken breast
Salt and pepper, to taste
1½ slices white bread
½ cup (100 ml) milk
¾ cup (180 ml) crème fraîche or heavy cream

*For the egg wash:*
1 egg yolk
1 teaspoon sugar

Add enough water to cover the bones, add the ½ chicken bouillon cube and simmer for 40 minutes until the liquid is reduced by half. Season with salt and pepper.

While the stock is simmering, you can prepare the puff pastry, duxelles, and fillets.

After about 40 minutes, pour the stock though a fine mesh strainer into a small saucepan. There should be only 2–2½ fl oz (60–70 ml) of cooking liquid remaining. Store in the refrigerator.

*The fillets:* Heat the vegetable oil and butter in a roasting pan. Salt and pepper the fillets and sear them in the hot oil over high heat just long enough to brown them evenly on all sides. Remove from the pan and set on a plate while you continue to prepare the duxelles, stuffing, puff pastry and the simmering stock.

*The duxelles:* Chop the mushrooms. In a sauté pan, cook the shallots in the butter for 2–3 minutes over moderate heat. Add the mushrooms, season with salt, turn the heat up high, and cook just until all the liquid has evaporated. Season with pepper and store in the refrigerator.

*The chicken stuffing: ‡* Chop the raw chicken meat in a food processor with the salt and pepper. Soak the bread in milk. Drain off the excess milk, add the bread to the chicken, and process the mixture. Add the cream by halves, processing to incorporate. Adjust the seasoning, adding salt and pepper as needed.

Combine half of the stuffing with the cold duxelles and store in the refrigerator. (See "Chef's suggestion" on uses for remaining half).

*The egg wash:* In a bowl stir the egg yolk, sugar, and 2 tablespoons cold water with a fork.

Divide the puff pastry into 4 equal sections. With a rolling pin, roll out each section into a rectangle 1/16–1/8-inch (2 mm) thick, and slightly wider than the fillets.

Spread a layer of the stuffing-duxelles mixture lengthwise in the center of 2 of the rectangles, spreading it about the size

of the fillets. Place a fillet over each rectangle of stuffing and cover with another thin layer of stuffing. Brush egg wash around the borders of the dough and place the second rectangle of dough on top. Seal and crimp the two layers of dough by pressing them gently together.

Make a chimney in the center of each rectangle by making a hole ½ inch (1 cm) in diameter. Slide a cylinder of parchment paper or aluminum foil into each hole.

With a pastry brush, glaze the dough with the egg wash. Place the puff pastry covered fillets on a baking sheet (either nonstick or slightly moistened with water). Refrigerate.

**30 minutes before serving:** Brush the dough with a second layer of egg wash. Preheat the oven to 400°F (200°C). Place the puff pastry-covered fillets in the oven for 15-20 minutes. Reheat the lamb stock over a hot water bath or double boiler.

*All the rich aroma of this marriage of lamb and mushrooms is retained—imprisoned in a sumptuous golden crust.*

**Just before serving:** Incorporate 2 tablespoons (30 g) of butter, cut into small pieces, whisking it into the hot lamb stock. Pour the sauce into a hot sauce boat.

Present the fillets on 2 cutting boards. Place the the 2 boards on large platter, and bring them triumphantly to the table.

**Chef's suggestions:** To assure success when preparing the puff pastry dough, it is necessary to make a larger quantity than is called for. Half the dough will be left over. You can freeze it, as the dough retains all its quality when defrosted in the refrigerator or at room temperature.

†It is difficult to prepare less than the given amount of chicken stuffing at a time. The surplus can be put in ramekins placed in a baking pan filled with enough hot water to come halfway up the sides of the ramekins. Bake for 20 minutes in an oven preheated to 300°F (150°C). These little chicken pâtés can be stored in the refrigerator for several days. You can serve them to accompany an apéritif; cut them into circles or squares and place them on small slices of toast spread with mustard. They can also be used to garnish a meat dish: Reheat them in a hot water bath and nap them with the same sauce made for the meat. All this is so good that you could even prepare twice as much stuffing as I have indicated!

**Chef's tip:** To obtain a uniform thickness when rolling out the dough, refer to the "Chef's tip" on page 85.

**Wine suggestions:** This is the moment to uncork a great Bordeaux, such as a Margaux or Pauillac (Médoc) aged several years and served *chambré* at 60°F (16°C), but no warmer.

*At the height of the season, this dessert, along with the countryside in the background, creates a harmony of tender pinks and greens (following page).*

# Le soufflé glacé aux fraises
## (Frozen Strawberry Soufflés)

~

**Shopping:** *Choose the freshest strawberries available, and save the very best for the garnish. Frozen strawberries turn into mush as soon as they thaw. On the other hand, you can use frozen raspberries, which still look good when defrosted at room temperature.

†The cocoa powder should be 100% pure cocoa, free of sugar or any other additives. It bears no resemblance to the chocolate powders used for breakfast drinks or hot chocolate mixes.

**The day before or several hours in advance:** At least 1 hour before, put the crème fraîche in a bowl in the refrigerator.

Wash, drain, and hull the strawberries. Put 6 of the nicest

Preparation: 50 minutes
Cooking: 5 minutes

Ease: Difficult
Cost: Moderate
Yield: 6 servings

Ingredients:
1 cup (250 g) crème fraîche
¾ lb (350 g) strawberries or
raspberries *

(Continued on page 98)

4 egg whites
1 pinch salt
1 cup (250 g) sugar
2 tablespoons cocoa powder †

berries intended for the garnish in the refrigerator. Purée the remainder. Push the purée through a fine mesh strainer held over a bowl and store in the refrigerator.

Put the egg whites and 1 pinch of salt in the bowl of an electric mixer fitted with the whisk attachment.

Combine the sugar and 10 tablespoons of water in a very clean saucepan. Cook over high heat. Immediately start whipping the egg whites, starting slowly. Increase the speed when the egg whites begin to foam. Meanwhile, keep an eye on the syrup. Cook it to 250°F (120°C), which ideally should be reached when the egg whites have taken on very firm peaks (see "Chef's tips," page 85). At this moment, lower the speed on the mixer and gradually pour the cooked syrup in a fine stream into the egg whites. Continue whipping the meringue until it is cool. Store it in the refrigerator.

Whip the well-chilled crème fraîche with an electric mixer for about 5 minutes. Stop whipping as soon as the cream forms firm peaks. Refrigerate the whipped cream so it does not break down.

Cut 6 strips of parchment paper 2½ inches (7 cm) wide and wrap them around ramekins 3–3½ inches (8–9 cm) in diameter and 1½ inches (4 cm) tall. Secure the paper with a rubber band or scotch tape; the paper gives extra height to the ramekins. Place them in the refrigerator or freezer.

When the meringue has completely cooled, fold half of the strawberry purée into it. Fold the remaining half of the purée into the whipped cream. Fold the two mixtures together, working from the bottom upward with a spatula. Pour the mixture into the ramekins so it is flush to the top of the edge of the parchment paper. Place the filled ramekins in the freezer for 5–6 hours.

**1 hour before serving:** Take the soufflés out of the freezer and place them in the refrigerator.

**Just before serving:** Remove the paper from around the ramekins. Dust the tops of the soufflés with cocoa powder. Dust the 6 strawberries with confectioners' sugar and place one on top of each soufflé.

**Chef's tips:** How do you know when the sugar syrup has reached 250°F (120°C)? The most simple way is to use a candy thermometer. If you do not have one available, set a bowl with water and ice cubes near the cooking sugar. When the sugar syrup is boiling and starts to form large bubbles, put a few drops into the bowl of ice water with a spoon. Try to pick up the syrup between two fingers. If you can form a small, soft ball, the sugar is ready.

To attractively dust the cocoa powder and confectioners' sugar, I put them, separately, in a small fine mesh strainer. Holding the strainer above the dish to be garnished, I stir with a spoon so the cocoa powder or confectioners' sugar falls gently and evenly.

**Wine suggestion:** After all, this is a party! Therefore, serve this dessert with a well-chilled Sauternes, 46–48°F (8–9°C).

# UN DÎNER À MOUGINS
## (DINNER AT THE MOUGINS)

~

*La tourte d'olives mouginoise*
*(Mougins-Style Olive Tart)*

*Les cuisses de poulet en court-bouillon de citron*
*(Chicken Legs with Aromatic Vegetables and Lemon)*

*Les tartelettes aux fruits du temps*
*(Seasonal Fruit Tartlets)*

~

*There is simplicity and sumptuous fragrance when the small black Niçoise olive marries with wild thyme.*

One day, an old man from Mougins told me, "You know, dear fellow, in the very place your restaurant is standing, there used to be a beautiful olive-oil windmill. When we worked nearby, or when we didn't have much to do, we came from time to time to see the miller. We always carried two or three garlic cloves and a knife in our pocket. We would gather several dandelions along with their roots because, don't forget, the root is the best part of the dandelion! We washed them in the brook as we passed by, and arriving near the millstone, we always found a leftover round of stale week-old bread.

"The miller gave us a *pignate* or crock filled with olive oil that had just flowed off the millstones. We rubbed the bread with garlic, dipped it in the pignate and chewed all this along with the dandelions and coarse salt. Add to this a shot of our wine from the hills! And so you see, my little one, I am not sure your clients relish all your complicated stuff as much as we did that very simple food. Anyway, to your health all the same!"

The moulin in which I installed my restaurant is beautiful and has certainly been there since the year 1500. It was while nostalgically thinking back on this unintentional gastronome that I created the olive tart. The other recipes on this menu are also prepared with regional products, simple, economical, and in season. You must always listen to the lessons of the elderly.

*The* pastis *can be prepared in the kitchen, but not in advance; it must be drunk in small sips as soon as it is ready.*

**For the apéritif:** You can always serve a small glass of well-chilled dry white wine or rosé, but *pastis* seems to me to be the outstanding choice. To properly appreciate it, prepare it according to the rules of the art of serving *pastis.* First, put no more than 1 or 2 ice cubes in a glass. Then pour one part *pastis* over the ice cubes. Finally, add, 4 parts water, very cold but not iced, about 43–45°F (6–7°C). The *pastis* can be further diluted with more water, but do not use any less. Above all, it is important to find a great *pastis.* The well-known and cheaper brands are simplified versions of the artisanal apéritif people concocted in the past according their own particular recipes (in secret, of course) after a long walk of picking herbs from the *garrigue.* The regional brands, less well-known (and a bit more expensive), offer anew the old-style *pastis,* obtained from infusions and liquors distilled from 10 or more different plants and spices. Their excellent quality amply justifies the price difference and they can often be found at a good wine store.

# La tourte d'olives mouginoise
## (Mougins-Style Olive Tart)

~

**Shopping:** *For the green leafy vegetables, the weight given here is based on cleaned leaves weighed after removing the white ribs from the Swiss chard and the chicory and the stems from the spinach.

**Everything can be prepared the day before:** Put the flour, ½ cup of the olive oil, 10 tablespoons tepid water, and salt in a bowl. Knead until the dough no longer sticks to the sides of the bowl and your hands. Slightly flatten the dough and refrigerate it for 30 minutes.

Chop the onions and sweat them in the remaining olive oil in a sauté pan over low heat. Stir occasionally and cook until tender and very lightly golden brown.

Meanwhile, wash, drain, and chop the leafy greens. Add them to the cooked onions along with the garlic and thyme flowers. Cook uncovered until all the cooking liquid has evaporated.

Pit the olives; if they are large, cut them in quarters.

In a large bowl, beat the eggs with the heavy cream. Off the heat, pour the cream-egg mixture into the pan with the vegetables. Blend well and give a few turns with the pepper mill. (The olives are salty enough that no additional salt should be necessary.)

Preheat the oven to 475°F (250°C). With your hands, pull the dough over a baking sheet into a disk 12 inches (30 cm) in diameter. Roll the edge of dough over and lift it up to form a ½-inch (5 mm) high border. Spread the vegetables evenly over the dough with a fork. Scatter the olives on top and bake for 25–30 minutes.

Preparation: 50 minutes
Cooking: 30 minutes

Ease: Easy
Cost: Inexpensive
Yield: 6 servings

Ingredients:
1 cup (250 g) flour
¾ cup tablespoons olive oil
1 pinch salt
½ lb (200 g) onions
1 lb (500 g) Swiss chard, spinach, or chicory *
6½ oz (180 g) small black olives
3 garlic cloves, finely chopped
½ teaspoon thyme flowers
2 eggs
2 tablespoons heavy cream
Pepper, to taste

*The delicious Nyons olive, always black, is harvested by hand in the dead of winter when it has reached perfect maturity. Today it is the only olive that bears the title AOC (Appellation d'Origine Contrôlée), a guarantee of quality and regional authenticity.*

**Just before serving:** Feast on this tart, hot or cold, in the shade of an olive tree if you can find one nearby; if not, any tree will do and the tart will be just as good!

**Wine suggestions:** Choose a dry white or rosé wine with a Côtes-de-Provence appellation. Or try a light and fresh red wine from the same year, such as a Gamay de Savoie or a Coteaux-du-Lyonnaise. Or why not champagne? Sometimes luxury can be a good thing! All these wines should be served well chilled at 46–50°F (8–10°C).

# Les cuisses de poulet en court-bouillon de citron
### (Chicken Legs with Aromatic Vegetables and Lemon)

~

Preparation: 45 minutes
Cooking: 45 minutes

Ease: Easy
Cost: Very economical
Yield: 6 servings

Ingredients:
6 large chicken legs with thighs, about ½ lb (200 g) each, or 6 chicken quarters
Salt and pepper, to taste
2 ripe tomatoes
3 lemons *
¾ cup extra-virgin olive oil
4 or 5 (300 g) medium carrots
1 large white onion
1 leek, white only

**Shopping:** *Try to find organic lemons that have not been sprayed. If unavailable, wash non-organic lemons well with warm water.

**Everything can be prepared several hours in advance:**
Prepare the chicken legs. Make a shallow cut into the joint between the thigh and the drumstick. With a knife, scrape and release the meat at the end of the drumstick. Cut off the end of the drumstick bone with a sturdy chef's knife. Salt and pepper the chicken legs (drumstick and thigh), and arrange them flat in one layer, so they do not overlap, in a baking pan.

Cover each chicken leg with 2 slices of tomato and 2 slices of lemon, alternating and overlapping the slices. Drizzle a bit of the olive oil over the chicken legs, tomatoes, and lemons.

Preheat the oven to 425°F (220°C).

Peel all the vegetables. Cut the carrots, onion, and leek into thin slices. Cut the celery and red pepper into short thin strips. Pour 4–5 tablespoons of olive oil in a sauté pan and add vegetables. Cook over moderate heat without browning, stirring occasionally.

When the vegetables are only slightly resistant to the bite, add ½ cup (100 ml) water and the wine. Add the bouquet garni, chicken bouillon cubes, and garlic.

Place the coriander seeds and peppercorns in a small piece of cheesecloth, tie the cloth with a string to form a small sachet, and put it into the pan with the vegetables. Cover the pan and cook for 20 minutes over low heat.

Roast the chicken for 20 minutes. Take it out of the oven but keep the oven on. Tilt the baking pan and skim off any rendered grease with a spoon.

Remove the bouquet garni from the pan of vegetables. Take out the peppercorn and coriander sachet and squeeze it over the pan to extract as much liquid as possible. Add 5 tablespoons olive oil and stir well. Spread the vegetables evenly over the chicken legs.

Return the pan to the oven for 20 minutes, lowering the temperature to 350°F (180°C).

Take the pan out of the oven, cover with aluminum foil, and set aside for at least 1 hour.

**Just before serving:** Remove the aluminum foil and add several thin slices of lemon and the chopped herbs: Parsley, chervil, and tarragon.

Serve the chicken at room temperature, no colder.

**Chef's suggestion:** I prefer to serve this dish with thick slices of buttered country bread to dip in the sauce. The ideal would be *fougassettes*, small Provençal breads made with olive oil. But if you do not live in the Midi (the south of France), it will no doubt be much easier to buy small round loaves or a country bread.

**Wine suggestion:** Don't drive yourself crazy! Stay with the same wine that you have chosen to accompany the first course.

1 celery stalk

½ red pepper

2 cups (500 ml) dry white wine

1 bouquet garni:

1 large bunch thyme, 1 bay leaf, and several parsley stems, all tied together

2 chicken bouillon cubes

2 garlic cloves, minced

1 tablespoon coriander seeds

1 teaspoon black peppercorns

1 small bunch parsley

1 small bunch chervil

12-15 fresh tarragon leaves

Salt and pepper, to taste

# Les tartelettes aux fruits du temps
## (Seasonal Fruit Tartlets)

~

**Several hours in advance:** Peel and cut into small pieces the orange, pear, apple, and peach. Place the fruit sections in a bowl and stir in the lemon juice to prevent browning.

Preheat an oven to 425°F (220°C).

Prepare the almond paste. In a large bowl, cream the butter for 1 minute with the ground almonds. Add ½ cup (100 g) of the sugar and blend well. Stir in the eggs.

Butter the bottom and sides of 6 tartlet molds 4 inches (10 cm) in diameter and pour in the almond paste. Bake for 15 minutes or until the paste is lightly browned.

Meanwhile, prepare a raspberry coulis. Crush all but 12 of the most attractive raspberries (for the garnish) in a food mill held over a bowl to catch the purée and juices. Save the raspberry seeds for later use. Add another ½ cup (100 g) of the sugar and stir well. Cover and store the coulis in the refrigerator.

Scrape the raspberry seeds out of the food mill into a small saucepan. Cook them with the remaining ½ cup (100 g) of sugar over low heat, stirring fairly often. Cook the mixture down into a jam.

Unmold the tartlets and spread them with a layer of the cooked raspberry seeds. Arrange the assorted cut fruit on top.

Heat the apple or quince jelly. Nap 1 tablespoon of jelly over each tartlet; as the jelly cools it will hold the fruits in place.

Decorate the tartlets with halved strawberries, the banana cut in slices, the remaining raspberries, small bunches of red currants or blueberries, and several mint leaves.

**Just before serving:** Pour a ring of raspberry coulis on 6 large flat plates. Place a tartlet in the center of each ring of coulis.

**Chef's suggestion:** Serve vanilla ice cream to accompany these tartlets, it's delicious!

Preparation: 40 minutes
Cooking: 25 minutes

Ease: Easy
Cost: Moderate
Yield: 6 servings

Ingredients:

1 orange

1 pear

1 apple

1 peach

Juice of 1 large lemon

1 stick (115 g) butter, softened

½ cup (115 g) ground almonds

1½ cups (300 g) sugar

3 eggs

10½ oz (300 g) raspberries

1 jar apple or quince jelly

6 strawberries

½ banana

2½ oz (75 g) red currants or blueberries

1 bunch mint

*Freshness, sweetness, fragrance, and lusciousness: all these qualities are combined in these dazzling tartlets.*

# LE DÎNER DE MA TANTE CÉLESTINE

## (AUNT CÉLESTINE'S DINNER)

~

*Les biscuits de loup à l'estragon*
*(Terrines of Tarragon-Flavored Sea Bass)*

*Les pigeons aux petits pois en cocotte*
*(Casserole of Pigeon with Small Peas)*

*La charlotte légère d'abricots*
*(Light Apricot Charlotte)*

~

*Peach-flavored champagne was Aunt Célestine's preferred cocktail: Peel and purée 2 white peaches, and strain. Add 2 tablespoons sugar and 1 teaspoon lemon juice. Store in the refrigerator. Just before serving, pour the peach purée into a carafe and add 1 bottle well-chilled champagne.*

My Aunt Célestine hosted a dinner party as though it were a holiday: Her pleasure began from the moment she sent the invitations. It then inflated during the shopping, persisted with the preparation of the meal, and finally reached its apotheosis in the happy smiles around the table. For Aunt Célestine, planning a dinner was a succession of small holidays that could last for several days, all for the sole pleasure of pleasing others.

This, I believe, is how parties should be given. An invitation should not be extended as though it represented a series of constraints, efforts, and chores. If your guests see how pleased you are to receive them, how carefully you attend to their well-being and the harmony of being together, what does it matter if something unexpected arises, any hitches, or even a recipe that isn't altogether successful? You will all laugh together!

As soon as the door is opened, your task consists of sweeping aside your friends' worries. Here is a tip to help you (this is what Aunt Célestine did): Drink a small glass of good wine or champagne just before your guests arrive. Your welcoming smile will already have an air of festivity.

# Les biscuits de loup à l'estragon
## (Terrines of Tarragon-Flavored Sea Bass)

~

Preparation: 30 minutes

Cooking: 25 minutes

Ease: Moderate

Cost: Fairly expensive

Yield: 6 servings

Ingredients:

¾ lb (375 g) sea bass fillets

Salt and pepper, to taste

7 egg yolks

10 tablespoons (150 g) butter

5 fl oz (170 ml) créme fraîche

(or heavy cream)

25 tarragon leaves


*For the Nantais butter:*

3 tablespoons wine vinegar

½ cup (100 ml) dry white

wine

1 oz (30 g) shallots, finely

chopped

1 teaspoon pepper, very

coarsely ground

1½ tablespoons crème fraîche

(or heavy cream)

12 tablespoons (180 g) butter

Salt, to taste

*Sea bass, nicknamed "wolf fish" due to its reputation for being ferocious, is the most highly esteemed Mediterranean fish.*

**Several hours before the meal:** Prepare the farce. Grind ½ lb (225 g) of the sea bass fillets in a food processor fitted with the blade attachment. Season with salt and pepper. Add the egg yolks and process for a few seconds. While the processor is running, quickly incorporate 10 tablespoons (150 g) softened butter and 5 fl oz (150 ml) crème fraîche (or cream). You should obtain a smooth paste-like consistency.

Cut the remaining fish fillets on an angle into 6 long narrow strips about the size of a pinky finger.

Butter 6 small (individual-sized) terrines with covers, or 6 ramekins. In each, place one strip of fish rolled into a spiral. Season with salt and pepper and sprinkle each mold with 4-5 tarragon leaves. Fill the molds with the farce spreading it slightly higher in the center into a dome and smoothing it with a spatula. Brush or sprinkle the surface with melted butter so the farce does not dry out during cooking. Cover with plastic wrap and refrigerate.

**40 minutes before serving:** Preheat the oven to 350°F (170°C). Place the terrines in a baking pan, adding enough water to come halfway up the sides of the terrines.

Set the pan over high heat. At first boil, place the pan in the oven and cook for 8 minutes. Cover, either with lids or aluminum foil, and cook for 12 more minutes.

Meanwhile, prepare the Nantais butter. In a stainless-steel saucepan, combine the vinegar, white wine, shallots, and pepper. Bring to a boil, then lower the heat and simmer until only 1 tablespoon of liquid remains. Add 1½ tablespoons crème fraîche (or cream). Bring back to a boil and briskly whisk in 12 tablespoons butter cut into small pieces, stir constantly until all the butter is melted and emulsified. Salt to taste. Pour through a fine mesh strainer. Keep warm in a hot water bath.

**Just before serving:** Put a folded napkin on an attractive platter. Place the terrines on top. Present the Nantais butter in a hot sauce boat.

At the table, in front of your guests, turn the terrines out onto hot plates and nap them with the Nantais butter.

**Chef's tip:** Sometimes I lighten and aerate the Nantais butter by blending it in the food processor with the blade attachment just before serving.

**Wine suggestion:** I would gladly uncork a fruity, dry white wine such as a Condrieu (northern Côtes-du-Rhône) for its apricot and peach notes, aged no more than 2 years.

## Les pigeons aux petits pois en cocotte
### (Casserole of Pigeon with Small Peas)

~

Preparation: 20 minutes
Cooking: 1 hour

Ease: Fairly easy
Cost: Moderate
Yield: 6 servings

Ingredients:
3 pigeons, about 1 lb
(500 g) each
9 tablespoons (130 g) butter
1½ shallots, chopped
1 cup (220 ml) white wine
¾ cube chicken bouillon
3 thyme sprigs
1 large bay leaf

*(Continued on next page)*

**Shopping:** *Of course it is always best to use peas freshly hulled from the pod; but out of season do not hesitate to use small frozen or canned peas.
†Use salted, preferably not smoked, bacon sliced ¼-inch (½-cm) thick and cut into ½-inch (1 cm) wide pieces.

**Several hours in advance:** Ask your butcher to truss the pigeons (or do it yourself) and to include the giblets on the side, not in the cavities.

Prepare a pigeon *jus* (a light sauce make with cooking juices) with the necks and wing tips. Brown them in a saucepan with 3 tablespoons (40 g) butter. Add the shallots and cook until golden brown. Pour in the wine and simmer until reduced by half.

Pour in cold water level to the bones and add the bouillon cube, thyme, bay leaf, and tomato paste. Simmer over low heat. When only 6 tablespoons of cooking liquid remain, pour it through a fine mesh strainer into a bowl.

Preheat the oven to 450°F (240°C).

1½ tablespoons tomato paste

Salt and pepper, to taste

3⅓ lbs (1.5 kg) young peas *

6 oz (200g) slab bacon,† cut

into about 25 cubes

30 pearl onions

3 pinches sugar

12 lettuce leaves

1½ cups (200 g) flour

*This is a delicious way to celebrate young, tender, vegetables of spring.*

Heat another 3 tablespoons (50 g) butter in a sauté pan. Salt and pepper the cavity and the outside of the pigeons. Brown the pigeons lightly on all sides in the butter. Put them in the oven for 12 minutes. During this time, baste the pigeons at least twice with the cooking juices.

Meanwhile, cook the peas for 3 minutes in boiling salted water. Put the bacon pieces in a small saucepan of cold water. Bring to a boil and cook for 2 minutes. Rinse and strain.

In a saucepan, heat the pearl onions with 1½ tablespoons (20 g) of butter, salt, pepper, sugar, and 5 fl oz (150 ml) water. Boil over high heat until nearly all the water has evaporated.

Set aside the vegetables and bacon, keeping them separate, on a large plate.

Put the lettuce leaves in a saucepan with 1½ tablespoons (20 g) of butter and cook them over moderate heat until tender. Add the bacon, pearl onions, and peas. Season with salt and pepper. Pour the entire contents into a heavy (such as cast-iron or enamel) casserole. Place the pigeons on top, douse them with the liquid in the bowl, and cover.

Prepare the dough to *luté* (seal) the casserole. Knead the flour with a little cold water, adding just enough to obtain a fairly soft dough. Roll the dough into a cylindrical strip and wrap it around the casserole between the cover and rim to seal the joint and prevent any steam from escaping during cooking.

**35 to 40 minutes before serving:** Preheat the oven to 400°F (200°C). Put the casserole in the oven for 20 minutes.

**Just before serving:** Bring the casserole to the table. In front of your guests break the beautifully browned crust made to *luté* the casserole. Gently lift up the cover and breathe in the aromas.

Cut the pigeons in half. Place each half on a hot plate, surround the pigeons with the vegetables, sprinkle with the cooking juices, and serve.

**Wine suggestions:** Stay classic by uncorking a good Bordeaux such as a Saint-Émilion or Saint-Estèphe, served *chambré*, at 60°F (16°C).

*To properly cook the pigeons, use a thick-bottomed casserole (such as black cast-iron or enamel), in which they should just fit, with a heavy, tight-fitting cover.*

# La charlotte légère d'abricots
## (Light Apricot Charlotte)

~

**Shopping:** *This recipe will be that much better if you can get hold of small muscat apricots. Though smaller and less attractive then other types, they are so delicious. Out of season, or if you simply can't find fresh ripe apricots, use canned apricots. In this case cut down the sugar to 1½ cups (300 g), and do not cook the apricots in syrup. Start the recipe at the point where the apricots are puréed with a quarter of the syrup, using the syrup from the can.

**The day before:** Put the crème fraîche in a large bowl, cover with plastic wrap, and refrigerate. Wash and stem the apricots, but do not pit them. Put them in a large saucepan with ½ cup (100 g) of the sugar, adding just enough cold water to cover the apricots. Place a plate inside the saucepan to weigh down the fruits so they are fully submerged in the water. Bring to a boil over high heat. At the first boil, turn off the heat, cover the saucepan, and set the apricots aside to poach for 15 minutes.

Pit the apricots. Put the apricots and a quarter of the syrup in a food processor fitted with the blade attachment or in a food mill with a fine screen. Purée. Add more syrup if the compote seems extremely thick.

Put half of the compote in the refrigerator. Pour the other half in a medium saucepan with the powdered milk. Stir to blend, and heat to a simmer.

Dissolve the powdered gelatin according to package directions, letting it stand a minute or two to soften. Whisk softened gelatin into the hot apricot mixture, off the heat, until dissolved.

In a large bowl, whisk the egg yolks and another ½ cup (100 g) of the sugar. Bring the compote to a simmer, then whisk it into the egg yolk-sugar mixture. Put the entire mixture into the saucepan and cook over very low heat, whisking constantly.

Preparation: 1 hour
Cooking: 20 minutes

Ease: Somewhat difficult
Cost: Inexpensive
Yield: 6 servings

Ingredients:

1 pint (250 ml) crème fraîche
(or 1⅓ cup heavy cream),
well-chilled
2 lbs (1 kg) ripe apricots *
2 cups (400 g) sugar
3 tablespoons powdered milk
½ tablespoon (8 g) powdered
gelatin
6 egg yolks
3 egg whites
20 ladyfingers, (approx.)
10 tablespoons apricot
liqueur

*Light in texture but
ebullient in flavor,
this sun-colored
charlotte deserves to
be served on plates
with a beautiful floral
pattern such as these.*

As soon as the mixture has thickened, but before it comes to a boil (do not allow this mixture to come to a boil or the eggs will curdle), pour it into a large bowl moistened with water. Set aside to cool, whisking occasionally, until the mixture is barely warm.

Whip the heavy cream with an electric beater for about 5 minutes, until it is firm and well aerated. Cover and refrigerate.

Whip the egg whites with 1 tablespoon of sugar to firm peaks.

Put 1½ oz (50 ml) water and 1 cup (200 g) sugar in a small saucepan over low heat. Have a bowl of cold water and ice cubes ready near the saucepan. When the syrup begins to thicken, occasionally pour a few drops of the syrup into the iced water with a spoon. As soon as you are able to lift the syrup up out of the water and form a soft ball between your thumb and fingers, take the syrup off the heat. Turn the electric beater on medium and slowly pour the syrup in a fine stream into the whipping egg whites. Continue whipping until the meringue is cool. Cover and refrigerate the meringue.

Cut the ladyfingers 2 inches (5 cm) long. Sprinkle the flat sides with 8 tablespoons apricot liqueur.

Cover the bottom of a cake pan 8–8½ inches (20–22 cm) in diameter with a circle of parchment paper. Line the sides of the cake pan with the ladyfingers standing upright, flat sides facing in.

Combine the apricot mixture and the well-chilled whipped cream and meringue, folding from the bottom upward with a rubber spatula. Carefully scrape all the way down into the bowl to fully blend all ingredients.

Fill the cake pan with the mousse flush to the rim of the mold. Smooth the top of the surface with a large flat metal spatula. Place the charlotte in the refrigerator for at least 6 hours.

**Just before serving:** Turn out the charlotte onto a chilled round cake platter. Coat the top of the charlotte with a thin layer of the reserved apricot compote. Pour 2 tablespoons of apricot liqueur into the remaining compote and present it on the side in a chilled sauce boat.

**Improvise!** Sometimes I flavor the apricots with vanilla by adding a vanilla bean, split lengthwise, to the water and sugar in which the apricots are poached. Also, for a change, I sometimes replace the apricot liqueur with a good French kirsch.

**Chef's suggestion:** If there is any apricot compote left over, put it in an airtight container. It can be stored for up to 3–4 days in the refrigerator.

**Decorating suggestion:** Wrap the base of the charlotte with a satin ribbon and bow.

**Wine suggestion:** I love to eat this charlotte with a small glass of *rasteau* (a naturally sweet wine from the Rhône valley). Serve it chilled, but not too cold, about 50–54°F (10–12°C).

*There is no longer a need for the small hammer that was used to break apart sugar loaves. On the other hand, the sugar shaker is a useful and elegant tool for evenly dusting confectioners' sugar on desserts.*

# AUTOUR D'UN
# NAVARIN PRINTANIER
## (A SPRING FEAST)

~

*Les frisures d'œufs en salade mouginoise*
*(Mouginoise Salad)*

*Le navarin d'agneau printanier*
*(Spring Lamb Stew with Baby Vegetables)*

*Le gratin d'abricots aux amandes, sirop de kirsch*
*(Apricot and Almond Gratins with Kirsch Syrup)*

~

*Lamb, eggs, fresh herbs, and spring vegetables: this menu contains all the symbols of Easter.*

At the farmers' market in the month of May, springtime is apparent on all the stands with their displays of tender young spring vegetables in soft colors, often tied together in bunches with their greenery still attached. In the past, when sheep were raised according to the seasons, spring was also the moment when lambs, born around Christmas, were in their prime and ready to be successfully prepared for the best dishes.

As for myself at this time, I can never resist the craving to lovingly prepare a *navarin* (lamb stew), an old classic of French cuisine. According to legend, its origin stems to the victory of the Franco-Anglo–Russian War of 1827 aboard the Turkish-Egyptian naval fleet at Navarin, in Greece. But I am quite sure that the recipe is even older and that its name is derived from the turnips (*navets* in French) that constitute the essential garnish.

It doesn't bother me a bit that this dish is not a new creation; on the contrary, in cooking, as in music, the most recent pieces often only survive for the length of a season. A great dish, like Bizet's *Carmen*, that voyages through centuries, lending itself to interpretations more or less successful, always rests

119

Fromage blanc *(a fresh light cow's cheese) is in season! Offer it for nibbling on toasts along with the apéritif. The day before, whip 1¾ cup (400 g)* fromage blanc, *well drained, with 1 small white onion, 1 grated garlic clove, 1 tablespoon strong mustard, salt, and pepper. Whip 3½ fl oz (100 ml) very cold crème fraîche (or heavy cream) to firm peaks. Fold the whipped crème fraîche into the cheese. In a fine mesh strainer set over a bowl, leave mixture to drain in the refrigerator for 12 hours. Just before serving, liberally sprinkle with finely chopped parsley and chives.*

on the knowledge, modesty, and deep understanding of its basic art. Enduring recipes remain the emblem of the *cuisine-vérité* by enhancing the value of the season and the freshness of the products.

Here is my version of a *navarin printanier*. To prepare it is as I do, if you do not have a vegetable garden, try to find the youngest, smallest, and most freshly picked vegetables possible. It really will make a difference. When you savor this country dish, you will not regret the time you spent to prepare it.

**For the apéritif:** Surprise your guests, Offer them a port from Xérès, a Fino (strong white and very dry) served at 50–52°F (10–11°C), or a Manzanilla, or even an Amontillado, served at the same temperature.

# Les frisures d'œufs en salade mouginoise
## (Mouginoise Salad)

~

**Several in advance:** Turn on the broiler. Place the red pepper under the broiler to char the skin, turning it occasionally so it blackens evenly.

Core the tomatoes and plunge them into a pot of boiling water for only a few seconds. Run them under cold water. Peel, cut into quarters, and remove the seeds. Reserve the center cores and seeds for the *navarin* (following recipe). Cut the quarters into strips. Put them in a colander and sprinkle with 1 teaspoon fine salt.

When the red pepper is charred all around, run it under cold water to remove the skin. Cut the pepper in half and seed it. Cut the halves into long strips and add them to the colander with the tomatoes.

Peel the cucumber and cut it lengthwise in long thin slices. Stop when you reach the seeds. Cut the slices into long strips. Add them to the colander with the tomatoes and red pepper. Sprinkle the entire mixture with a large pinch of coarse salt.

Preparation: 50 minutes

Cooking: 5–10 minutes

Ease: Easy

Cost: Inexpensive

Yield: 6 servings

Ingredients:

1 sweet red pepper

2 large tomatoes

1 teaspoon salt

1 cucumber

1 teaspoon coarse salt

5 eggs

7 tablespoons extra-virgin olive oil

1 tablespoon parsley, chopped

Salt and pepper, to taste

1 head of lettuce

1 garlic clove, chopped

2 anchovy fillets

1 teaspoon strong mustard

2 teaspoons wine vinegar

1½ oz (50 g) small black Niçoise olives

12 basil leaves

1 bunch chives

*The elegance of this dish depends entirely on the finesse of the omelettes.*

With a fork, whisk together the eggs, 2 tablespoons olive oil, parsley, salt, and pepper.

Lightly oil 2 nonstick crêpe pans and heat them over moderate heat. Pour a small ladle of the egg mixture in a thin even layer in the pan as if making a crêpe. Cook on both sides. Slide the omelette out of the pan onto a plate. Continue in this way until all the egg mixture is used up. Between making each omelette, wipe the pan with a paper towel moistened with oil.

Cut the omelettes into *chiffonade:* Roll up 3–4 omelettes (stacked on top of each other) into a tight spiral and slice the stack into thin strips. Cover and refrigerate.

**Just before serving:** Wash the lettuce. Cut the leaves in *chiffonnade* by stacking and rolling them into spirals and cutting them into thin strips as for the omelettes.

Prepare a vinaigrette: In a shallow bowl, crush the chopped garlic and anchovy fillets with a fork. Put them into a large bowl with the mustard, 1 pinch salt, and the vinegar. Slowly whisk in 5 tablespoons oil with a fork. Taste the vinaigrette and, if needed, add a pinch more of salt, being careful not to add too much (remember the anchovies are salty). Rinse the cucumber under cold water and drain it well. Add the cucumber, tomato, red pepper, and omelette *chiffonnade* to the bowl with the vinaigrette. Gently toss the ingredients.

Line the bottom of a second bowl with the lettuce *chiffonnade*. Mound the mixed salad ingredients on top. Scatter on the black olives, basil leaves, and chopped chives. Serve at room temperature, no colder.

**Wine suggestions:** Choose a white wine from Cassis or Arbois. Chill to 46–50°C (8–10°C) in an ice bucket with water and a few ice cubes.

*Use the best products of the season, and put them all together in a heavy casserole: this is one of the oldest dishes that makes up the grande cuisine.*

# Le navarin d'agneau printanier
## (Spring Lamb Stew with Baby Vegetables)

~

**Shopping:** The quality of the stew depends entirely on the vegetables. Choose them as small, fresh, and tender as possible. For the potatoes, I prefer new red potatoes or *rattes* for their texture and fragrance.

**Several hours in advance:** Prepare the *navarin*. Remove the thin membrane and fat on the lamb shoulders. Cut the meat off the bones in large cubes, about 2 inches square (5 cm).

Preparation: 45 minutes
Cooking: 1 hour, 25 minutes

Ease: Fairly easy
Cost: Moderately expensive
Yield: 6 servings

Ingredients:
*For the navarin:*
3 lamb shoulders, 2½–3⅓
lbs (1.2–1.5 kg) each
7 oz (200 g) carrot
7 oz (200 g) onion
1 large bunch parsley
1 large bunch thyme
1 bay leaf
1 lb (500 g) ripe tomatoes
1 head of garlic
1 tablespoon vegetable oil
1 tablespoon butter
1 tablespoon flour

*For the garnish:*
2 bunches baby carrots
2 bunches baby turnips
½ lb (200 g) small white
onions or green onions
1 lb oz (500 g) small
potatoes
1 lb (500 g) baby peas
⅔ lb (300 g) thin green beans

*The pleasure in preparing a navarin begins at the market when buying the most crisp, tender spring vegetables. Choose the freshest available.*

Peel the carrots and onions. Cut them into ½-inch (1 cm) cubes. Make a bouquet garni by tying together the parsley stems (reserve the leaves for later), half of the bunch of thyme, and the bay leaf.

Core the tomatoes and cut in half. Gently press on each half to squeeze out the seeds. Cut the tomato meat into cubes and set aside. If you prepared the Mouginoise Salad (previous recipe) for the first course, add the tomato cores reserved from this dish.

Peel and crush the garlic.

Preheat the oven to 250°F (120°C).

Heat 1 tablespoon oil and 1 tablespoon butter in a heavy casserole (black cast-iron or enamel). Salt the cubes of meat and put them in the hot casserole. Brown the meat evenly on all sides without letting it dry out. Take the meat out the casserole and drain it in a colander.

Without rinsing the casserole, add the cubed carrots and onions. Brown, stirring occasionally, then put them in the colander with the meat. Return the meat and vegetables to the casserole, add the crushed garlic and flour, and cook over moderate heat. Stir and cook for 1 minute. Add the bouquet garni and the tomatoes. Add water level with the ingredients. Cover and bring to a boil. Put the casserole in the oven, and cook at a simmer for 40 minutes.

Meanwhile, peel the garnish vegetables. Rinse them without soaking, except for the potatoes, which should be kept in a bowl of cold water.

Blanch the carrots in boiling salted water for 4 minutes. Do the same for the turnips for 5 minutes. Drain them in a colander.

Put the onions in a small saucepan with 1 pinch salt, 1 pinch sugar, and 1 tablespoon butter. Add water level with the onions. Simmer over moderate heat until all the water has evaporated.

Take the casserole out of the oven but keep the oven on. With a slotted spoon, remove the pieces of meat and put them on a plate. Cover with a sheet of aluminum foil and set aside in a warm area.

Pour the sauce through a fine mesh strainer held over a saucepan, discarding the strained carrots and onions. Cook the sauce at a boil for 5 minutes over moderate heat. Skim off any fat that rises to the surface. Add the carrots and turnips.

Cook the potatoes in boiling salted water for 2 minutes. Drain them.

Put the sauce, carrots, turnips, meat, onions, peas, and potatoes in the casserole. Season with salt and several turns of the pepper mill. Add the remaining thyme. Cover, bring to a boil, and place in the oven to cook for 20 minutes.

Cook the green beans until slightly crisp to the bite, and drain.

Coarsely chop the parsley.

Take the casserole out of the oven. Remove the thyme, sprinkle the *navarin* with the parsley and green beans, cover, and set aside.

**Just before serving:** While feasting on the first course, reheat the *navarin* over low heat. Present it in the casserole.

**Wine suggestion:** With this fresh dish, I love drinking an elegant and tasty young Bordeaux Saint-Estèphe served wine-cellar temperature, 50–53°F (10–12°C).

# Le gratin d'abricots aux amandes et au kirsch

## (Apricot and Almond Gratins with Kirsch Syrup)

~

**The day before:** Prepare the fruit. Place the whole apricots in a stainless-steel saucepan (the apricot pit gives an almond flavor to the apricots). In a second saucepan, bring 20 fl oz (600 ml) water, the vanilla bean, honey, and sugar to a boil. Pour the boiling syrup over the apricots. Bring the syrup back to a boil and take it off the heat. Cover the saucepan and set it aside for 24 hours, checking that the apricots are well submerged in the syrup. If necessary, place a plate upside-down in the saucepan to weigh down the apricots so they are immersed in the syrup.

**Several hours in advance:** Strain the apricots, cut them in half and pit them. Reserve the syrup. Set aside the most attractive apricot halves for garnish. Purée a quarter of the apricots with a little bit of the syrup to obtain a thick compote.

In a bowl, combine the ground almonds and sugar. Add the butter, whole egg, and egg yolks. Stir the mixture with a whisk to obtain a smooth texture.

Divide the apricot halves among 6 individual gratin dishes. Cover them with the almond cream. If the cream is too stiff, warm it very slightly to soften. Sprinkle the sliced almonds on top. Dust with confectioners' sugar.

**40 minutes before serving:** Preheat the oven to 400°F (210°C). Bake the gratins for 15-20 minutes until golden brown. Gently heat the apricot compote, and add the kirsch.

**Just before serving:** Place paper doilies on 6 small plates. Place the gratin dishes on top. Serve immediately, with the compote presented on the side in a sauce boat.

**Improvise!** Try replacing the apricots with peaches, pears, or even prunes. You can also use apricot brandy instead of kirsch.

Preparation: 30 minutes
Cooking: 20 minutes

Ease: Easy
Cost: Inexpensive
Yield: 6 servings

Ingredients:
*For the fruits:*
1 lb (1 kg) fresh apricots
1 vanilla bean
1 cup (200 g) honey
1 cup (200 g) sugar
2 tablespoons kirsch

*For the almond cream:*
5 oz (150 g) ground almonds
2/3 cup (150 g) sugar
10 tablespoons (150 g) butter, softened
1 egg
2 egg yolks
2 tablespoons (25 g) sliced almonds
2 tablespoons confectioners' sugar

# PARFUMS ET ÉPICES
## (SCENTS AND SPICES)

~

*La compote de poivrons doux aux anchois*
*(Roasted Sweet Red Pepper and Anchovy Compote)*

*La daurade royale rôtie à la sarriette et au gingembre*
*(Roasted Royal Sea Bream with Savory and Ginger-Orange Butter)*

*Les pêches ou poires au vin de poivre et de laurier*
*(Peaches or Pears Poached in Pepper and Bay Leaf-Scented Wine)*

~

This menu reflects the harmony of a life; the mingling of childhood memories with today's friendships and the richness of the sea and the land.

One day my friend Pierrot, a fisherman from Suquet (old Cannes), caught a beautiful royal sea bream weighing 3½ lbs (1.6 kg). We immediately decided to savor it under the most delicious conditions. We went on a tour through my garden to profit from its abundance and picked sweet peppers and savory, velvety peaches.

Afterward, seated at the table with a well-chilled bottle of rosé Bandol, we envisioned the entire menu. Pierrot is not only a fisherman without equal, but also a cordon-bleu!

Breathing in the deep, light scent of the peaches, I recalled a dessert my Aunt Célestine used to make. When I was quite young she often prepared a fruit soup similar to the one in this menu. Just before serving, she poured in a good sized glass of crème de cassis (black-currant liqueur). What was surprising was that while I wasn't allowed to eat the fruit, I was permitted a bit of this delicious syrup in which I dipped ladyfingers.

How could I possibly not become a gourmand with such an education!

**For the apéritif:** What could be more fragrant than a *pastis* clouded with ice and water. Don't forget to offer several black Niçoise olives and *picholines* (green Niçoise olives).

*The glorious color of sweet peppers, whether you prefer yellow or red, always gives dishes a tempting aspect.*

# La compote de poivrons doux aux anchois
## (Roasted Sweet Red Pepper and Anchovy Compote)

~

Preparation : 15 minutes

Cooking: approx. 30 minutes

Ease: Easy

Cost: Inexpensive

Yield: 6 servings

Ingredients:

6 sweet red peppers *

10 tablespoons (150 ml)
olive oil

½ teaspoon thyme flowers

3 garlic cloves

18 basil leaves

6 mint leaves

30 anchovy fillets, †
packed in oil

Pepper, to taste

12 slices country bread,
toasted (optional)

**Shopping:** *I recommend using large, meaty, sweet red peppers for this recipe. They should be firm, smooth, and shiny, without bruises.
†For the anchovy fillets, I prefer those from Collioure in the Roussillon region. This little coastal village has made them its specialty.

**The day ahead or morning before:** Turn on the broiler. Place the red peppers under the broiler to char the skin, turning them occasionally so they blacken evenly. You can also do this on the stovetop, if you have gas burners, over the flames. Once the skins are charred, run the peppers under cold water, rubbing them to remove the skin. Cut off the stems, cut the peppers in half lengthwise, and seed them. Cut the halves into strips.

Heat the olive oil in a small cast-iron or enameled casserole. Add the red peppers and thyme flowers. Cook gently for 15 minutes over low heat. Meanwhile, finely chop the garlic, basil, and mint.

Add the anchovy fillets to the casserole. Stir until they are melted, about 1–2 minutes. When the peppers are cooked, take them off the heat. Stir in the garlic, basil, and mint. Add pepper to taste. Transfer the mixture to a large bowl or earthenware platter.

Serve at room temperature, *but not chilled.* No, I have not forgotten the salt, the anchovies are salty enough.

**Chef's suggestion:** This compote can be eaten alone or with slices of toasted country bread, hard-boiled eggs, black Niçoise olives, or canned white tunafish packed in oil.

**Improvise:** To change the flavor and color of this dish, you can replace the red peppers with yellow peppers.

# La daurade royale rôtie à la sarriette et au gingembre

## (Roasted Royal Sea Bream with Savory and Ginger-Orange Butter)

~

**Shopping:** *The royal sea bream is one of the most noble salt-water fish. You can save a bit of money if you fish for it yourself. It can be recognized by its steel-gray color and slightly truncated pug-nosed snout topped by a slight golden bump. Ask the fish merchant to scale and gut it.
†Savory is also known as *pèbre d'ase* ("ass's pepper") at the Provençal farmers markets. ‡I prefer Thompson oranges for this recipe, as the oranges should be seedless.

**2 hours ahead:** Liberally salt and pepper the inside of the sea bream. Stuff it with several stems of savory and spread the remainder in an even layer on a baking dish. Place the fish on top of the savory and sprinkle it with oil. Put 3–4 tablespoons of water on the bottom of the dish, making sure it doesn't come in contact with the fish. Set the platter in a cool area, but not in the refrigerator.

Peel and finely grate the ginger. Grate the zest of ½ orange. Cut off the skin of the 3 oranges (see "Chef's tip," page 47).

Preparation: 20 minutes
Cooking: 35 minutes

Ease: Easy
Cost: Moderately expensive
Yield: 6 servings

Ingredients:
1 royal sea bream,* 4½–5½ lbs (2–2.5 kg)
Salt and pepper, to taste
1 bunch fresh savory †
8 tablespoons olive oil
3 oz (90 g) fresh ginger
3 oranges ‡
8½ tablespoons butter

*For variation, make a bold presentation: surround the sea bream with a row of orange sections and bay leaves.*

Section the oranges over a bowl to catch the dripping juices.

**50 minutes before serving:** Preheat the oven to 450°F (240°C).

**30 minutes before serving:** Bake the sea bream for 15 minutes (10 minutes for 2 smaller fish). Lower the temperature to 350°F (180°C) and cook for 20 minutes more. Check the dish: if the water has completely evaporated, add a bit more.

**Just before serving:** Put the reserved orange juice in a small saucepan with 1 pinch of salt. Bring to a boil. Cut the butter into small pieces and briskly whisk it into the boiling juice, stirring constantly until the sauce is perfectly emulsified.

Add the grated ginger and orange zest. Do not allow the sauce to boil. Put the orange sections in a sauce boat and pour the sauce on top. Season with salt and pepper to taste.

When the sea bream is cooked, present it on an attractive hot platter. Bring it to the table accompanied with the sauceboat of ginger-orange butter.

**Improvise!** The sea bream can be replaced with any other firm-fleshed saltwater fish such as red snapper or sea bass.

**Wine suggestions:** Choose a round, dry white wine, such as a Pouilly-Fumé (Loire) or a Hermitage, or a northern Côtes-du-Rhône white, a bit spicy with a complex nose. These wines should be served at 46–50°F (8–10°C).

*Roasted sea bream surrounded by the ingredients used in this recipe: orange, savory, and ginger.*

# Les pêches ou poires au vin de poivre et de laurier

(Peaches or Pears Poached in Pepper and
Bay Leaf-Scented Wine)

~

**Preparation:** 25 minutes
**Cooking:** 20 minutes

**Ease:** Easy
**Cost:** Moderate
**Yield:** 6 servings

**Ingredients:**
2 cups (500 ml) red port
3 cups (750 ml) red wine *
2 teaspoons black peppercorns
Peel of 1 lemon
1 vanilla bean
5 bay leaves †
5 tablespoons flower honey
12 vine peaches ‡ or 12 Williams pears

*The wine and port give white pears a beautiful brilliant purple color and a complex fragrance.*

**Shopping:** *Choose a wine rich in tannins and with a deep color, for instance a young Bordeaux, or other wine from the Southwest, such as young Cahors. †It is preferable to use fresh rather than dry bay leaves. They release a stronger, cleaner aroma, and do not crack as easily during cooking, so are more attractive when served. ‡Vine peaches are not easily available, and can be replaced with very fragrant medium white peaches.

**At least 2 hours ahead:** Pour the port and wine into a large saucepan. Put the peppercorns into a square of cheesecloth, gather the ends, and tie them to form a sachet. Put sachet in the wine along with the lemon peel, vanilla bean, and bay leaves. Bring to a boil. Remove from heat, add honey, and cover.

Put the peaches in a saucepan of boiling water for 2 minutes, then immediately submerge them in cold water and peel. (If you have chosen to make pears, peel them, keeping the stems attached.)

Just after peeling, put the fruit in the still-hot wine, and cook over high heat. At first boil, lower the heat and simmer for 10 minutes. Take the pan off the heat, cover, and set aside to cool.

Squeeze the liquid from the peppercorn sachet into the wine and stir to blend. Discard the sachet. Put the fruit and its cooking liquid in a bowl.

Retrieve the bay leaves and stick them on top of the peaches or pears as though they were leaves. To decorate the peaches, cut the vanilla bean into 12 sections and stick the pieces into the tops of the peaches as though they were stems.

Store the fruits in a cool area, but not in the refrigerator. The flavor of the pepper combined with the port will give a refreshing enough impression.

# MENU POUR DES COPAINS
## (A MENU FOR CLOSE FRIENDS)

~

*Le tourin d'ail doux*
*(Sweet Garlic Soup)*

*L'entrecôte de charolais à la fondue d'anchois et aux herbes*
*(Shell Steak with Anchovies and Herbs)*

*Les tartelettes aux pommes et aux noix*
*(Individual Apple Walnut Tarts)*

~

*In Provence, good friends never have a reunion without a game of* pétanque *(a type of lawn bowling). Even the chef, while waiting for the food to cook, can take the time to aim a* cochonnet *(the jack ball) between sips of* apéritif.

One day while waiting for my friend Émile, a pipe smoker, and not one to hold back when offered hard liquor, I was meditating over our menu. I had met Émile many years ago, going back to our hunts in Kenya. I was to compose a rather flamboyant menu that would gratify the solidity and warmth of his palace.

What could be better than a sweet garlic soup and beautiful steaks with anchovies?

A cook exercises great power over the health of his guests. When I prepare garlic soup I get the feeling of treating them with a good remedy for their ills.

When I was child I knew an elderly couple who amazed the village with their vivacity. This couple cultivated eight hundred garlic plants in their garden every year for their own personal use. With this they had enough to each consume one large head of garlic every day. I won't say they had particularly fresh breath, but they did live to be ninety years old and passed away, as we say, in perfect health! This is why it eases my conscience to serve garlic to a real gourmand such as Émile.

137

**For the apéritif:** Be different—transform the famous Canon kir into a Cardinal kir. Replace the Burgundy Aligoté with a Hermitage and the *crème de cassis* (black-currant liqueur) with a *crème de mûre* (blackberry liqueur). Use 1 teaspoon of liqueur for 3½ fl oz (100 ml) of wine. Accompany this apéritif with several slices of dry Arles sausage.

*One tablespoon of cassis in a small glass of well-chilled white vermouth and voilà, yet another idea for an easy-to-prepare, unusual fruity apéritif.*

# Le tourin d'ail doux
## (Sweet Garlic Soup)

~

**35 minutes before serving:** Peel the garlic cloves. Put them in a saucepan with 2 quarts (2 liters) cold water. Bring to a boil, and drain. Repeat this step: Change the water, bring to a boil, and drain.

Put the blanched garlic cloves back in the saucepan with 1 generous quart (1 liter) water, a pinch of salt, and the bouillon cubes. Bring to a boil, lower the heat, and cook for 7–8 minutes at a simmer.

When the garlic cloves are completely tender to the touch, add the bread crumbs. At the first boil, add the crème fraîche (or cream).

As soon as the soup comes back to a boil, pour it into a blender or food processor with the butter. Purée on high speed. Salt to taste and add a grind or two of fresh pepper.

Serve immediately in a hot soup tureen.

**Chef's suggestion:** If I serve this soup in individual bowls, I sometimes add a raw egg yolk to each bowl just before serving.

**Wine suggestion:** If you really want to drink wine with this thirst-quenching soup, uncork a robust, rugged-accented Cahors.

Preparation: 15 minutes
Cooking: 10 minutes

Ease: Easy
Cost: Inexpensive
Yield: 6 servings

Ingredients:
9 oz (250 g) garlic cloves
Salt and pepper, to taste
2 chicken bouillon cubes
5 oz (150 g) bread crumbs, without crust
1¼ cup (300 ml) crème fraîche (or heavy cream)
2 tablespoons (30 g) butter

# L'entrecôte de charolais à la fondue d'anchois et aux herbes
## (Shell Steak with Anchovies and Herbs)

~

Preparation: 10 minutes
Cooking: 10-15 minutes

Ease: Easy
Cost: Moderate
Yield: 6 servings

Ingredients:
10 tablespoons (150 g) butter
3 shell steaks,* 16–20 oz
(500–600 g) each
Salt and pepper, to taste
18 anchovy fillets,† packed
in olive oil
Juice of 1 lemon
1 teaspoon thyme flowers
1 teaspoon finely
chopped savory
2 heaping tablespoons
chopped parsley
1 teaspoon finely
chopped garlic
1 teaspoon Worcestershire
sauce

**Shopping:** *Request well marbleized steaks and ask the butcher to trim off all nerves and excess fat.
†If you prefer to use anchovies packed in salt, you can prepare them yourself. Rinse them with cold water or soak them for at least 30 minutes in a large bowl of cold water. Wipe and set aside to marinate for at least 12 hours in olive oil.

**15-20 minutes before serving:** Heat 2 large sauté pans with 1 tablespoon butter in each pan. Salt and pepper the steaks on both sides. When the butter is golden brown, put in the steaks. Cook them over moderate heat for 2–3 minutes on each side, according to your taste and the thickness and texture of the steaks.

When the steaks are cooked, take them out of the pan and place them on a small plate that has been set upside down on top of a large plate; this will prevent the meat from soaking in its drained juices. Cover the steaks with aluminum foil to keep them warm.

Discard the cooking juices from of one of the sauté pans, but do not wash it. Put in the anchovy fillets and cook them over low heat until melted. Add remaining butter and turn up the heat to medium. Add the lemon juice, thyme, savory, parsley, garlic, and Worcestershire sauce. Season liberally with a pepper mill, add the juices that have drained off the steaks. Heat gently without boiling.

Cut the steaks in half crosswise, place them on 6 hot plates, and generously nap them with the sauce.

**Wine suggestions:** Treat yourself to a vintage southern Côtes-du-Rhône such as a red Châteauneuf-du-Pape, aged 2–3 years and serve it at 57–59°F (14–15°C). Or, if you prefer, a red Collioure served at the same temperature.

# Les tartelettes aux pommes et aux noix
## (Individual Apple Walnut Tarts)

~

**Several hours in advance:** Preheat the oven to 350°F (180°C). Coarsely chop the walnuts with a knife. Cream the butter in a bowl. Add the sugar and cream it with the butter. Stir in the eggs one at a time, add the flour, and finally the walnuts.

Butter 6 tartlet molds, 3½–4 inches (9–10 cm) in diameter. Fill the molds with the batter. Peel the apples. Cut them in half, and core and seed them. Slice them thinly. Divide the apple slices among the tarts, overlapping them over the batter. Bake the tarts for about 20 minutes. Dust the tarts with confectioners' sugar, then return them to the oven for 5–10 minutes to brown. Place them on a cooling rack.

**Just before serving:** Slightly reheat the tarts in the oven until warm, not hot. Serve immediately.

**Improvise!** If reinette apples are not available, I replace them with 20 prunes cooked in wine. To cook the prunes, place them in a saucepan with 8 fl oz (250 ml) water and 8 fl oz (250 ml) wine, 2 tablespoons sugar, and the zest of one lemon. Simmer for 10 minutes on low heat. Drain the prunes and pit them. Place 3–4 prunes, depending on the size, in each tartlet mold filled with walnut batter. Bake and finish as indicated for the apple tarts above.

Preparation : 20 minutes
Cooking: 30–40 minutes

Ease: Easy
Cost: Inexpensive
Yield: 6 servings

Ingredients:
2½ oz (75 g) walnuts
10 tablespoons (150 g) butter, softened
5 oz (150 g) sugar
3 eggs
1 cup (150 g) flour
3 apples, preferably reinettes or Granny Smiths
⅓ cup (75 g) confectioners' sugar

*For variation, the same tart can be prepared with prunes cooked in wine.*

# UN DÉJEUNER D'AUTOMNE
## (AN AUTUMN LUNCHEON)

~

*La quiche crémeuse aux morilles*
*(Creamy Morel Quiche)*

*Les côtes de veau au pastis et aux pions d'ail*
*(Veal Chops with Anise and Garlic)*

*Le soufflé léger aux reinettes*
*(Light Reinette Apple Soufflé)*

~

The fragrances of the Midi can be married with those from the north in the same menu. Autumn, the crossroad of seasons and aromas, gladly lends itself to these vast harmonies.

That was the season when friends from the north passed by the Moulin one day in October. Before letting them return to their morose northern winter, I wanted to invigorate them with a menu from our area, one they could also prepare at home, by adding a ray of Provençal light to their cuisine.

And that is the basis for this menu, with the earthy woody fragrance of the morel quiche, the generosity of a beautiful veal chop, the sun filled vigor of the garlic strips, and a touch of *pastis* to help you take on the winter with courage.

*When the country-side, tired by the sun, begins to turn russet, the Provençal vines yield the grapes used to make the great white, rosé, and red wines.*

**For the apéritif:** It can be a bitter thing to leave the beautiful summer behind us, though we can appreciate the often neglected bitter flavors with which we can compose delicious apéritifs. So open a good bottle of white Côtes-de-Provence wine and add *crème de noix* (walnut liqueur), dosing it to your taste.

Autumn is also an auspicious time for mushrooms. Slice a few porcini and sauté them in a pan with olive oil and a bit of chopped shallots and parsley. Divide the mushrooms among slices of plain toasted baguette. Serve hot with well-chilled walnut-flavored wine, and you will go wild over this alliance between north and south.

*Make the most of the harvest season by putting summer in a jar, so all year long you can enjoy the aromas and vitamins offered by the sun.*

# La quiche crémeuse aux morilles
## (Creamy Morel Quiche)
~

**At least 8 hours in advance or the day before:** Prepare the dough. Put the flour, salt, butter (cut into small pieces), egg, and 5 tablespoons cold water in the work bowl of a food processor fitted the blade attachment. Blend the ingredients on low speed, adding a bit more cold water if the dough seems dry. As soon as the dough begins to come together, stop processing.

If you do not have a food processor, put the flour in a bowl and make an indentation in the center. Put the remaining ingredients in the indentation and work the flour into the center with your fingertips, kneading as little as possible, to bring the ingredients together into a ball.

Wrap the dough in plastic film and place it in the least cool section of the refrigerator to rest for at least 6 hours.

Roll out the dough $1/16$–$1/8$-inch (2 mm) thick. Line it in a tart mold 10 inches (25 cm) in diameter and 1 inch (3 cm) high. Allow the edges of the dough to extend over the sides of the mold, and cut off the excess by running a rolling pin over the rim of the mold. Store the trimmings (there will be a goodly amount) in plastic wrap in the refrigerator or freezer for another use.

Crimp the border of the tart shell between the thumb and index finger, raising it slightly. Prick the bottom of the shell with a fork. Put the shell in the freezer for at least 1 hour; this will prevent the dough from shrinking during baking.

**2 hours before serving:** Preheat an oven to 425°F (220°C). Cover the base of the shell with a circle of parchment paper and fill with the dried beans to just below the rim of the mold. Bake the shell for 15 minutes but don't let it brown. Remove the beans and paper. Place the shell on a cooling rack, keeping the tart shell in the mold.

If you are using dried morels, soak them in tepid water for 1 hour.

Preparation: 30 minutes
Cooking: 45 minutes

Ease: Easy
Cost: Expensive
Yield: 6 servings

Ingredients:
*For the dough:*
2 cups (300 g) flour
1 teaspoon salt
9 tablespoons (125 g) butter
1 egg
1 lb (500 g) dried beans

*For the filling and garnish:*
3 oz (90 g) dried morels or 14 oz (400 g) fresh morels
2 tablespoons (30 g) butter
2 tablespoons chopped shallots
$1\frac{1}{2}$ cups (350 ml) crème fraîche (or heavy cream)
Salt and pepper, to taste
2 eggs
2 egg yolks
2 tablespoons chopped chives
dash of ground nutmeg

**50 minutes before serving:** Preheat the oven to 400°F (200°C).

Drain the morels, squeezing on them gently to extract the excess water.

If you are using fresh morels, do not wash them, as they absorb too much water. Cut off the stem, which is often covered with soil. Blow on the tops to dislodge any traces of soil, and wipe with a moist kitchen towel.

Heat the butter in a sauté pan over high heat. Cook the shallots until lightly golden brown, add the morels. Stir occasionally and cook until any rendered water has evaporated.

Add ½ cup (125 ml) crème fraîche (or cream) and season with salt and pepper. Simmer for 4–5 minutes. Transfer the morels to a plate and set them aside.

Put the eggs and egg yolks in a bowl and whisk for 2 minutes. Whisk in the remaining crème fraîche, the chives, nutmeg, and salt and pepper. Blend well.

**30 minutes before serving:** Spread the morels and cream evenly over the bottom of the tart shell. Cover with the egg-cream mixture. Bake for 30 minutes.

The quiche is cooked when it is golden brown and the tip of a knife inserted in the center comes out almost clean. Present the tart on a round platter.

**Chef's suggestion:** You will yield extra dough with this recipe. Store it, wrapped in plastic film, for one week in the refrigerator, or longer in the freezer. It can be used to prepare pâtés, fruit tarts, or savory tartlets garnished with poached eggs and spinach, or asparagus tips, smoked salmon, etc.

**Chef's tip:** For even dough, refer to the "Chef's tip," page 85.

**Wine suggestion:** With this quiche I like to drink a Pouilly-Fumé (Loire white wine) from a good year, aged 2–3 years. Chill it to 46–48°F (8–9°C), no colder, to best enjoy the aromas produced by this Sauvignon grape variety.

*Fresh morels are mostly gathered in springtime. Dried, they are the mushrooms that reconstitute most successfully with regard to texture and fragrance. Their earthy, woody aroma is what makes them so well-loved for cooking during cold seasons.*

# Les côtes de veau au pastis et aux pions d'ail
## (Veal Chops with Anise and Garlic)

~

Preparation: 30 minutes

Cooking: 20 minutes

Ease: Easy

Cost: Expensive

Yield: 6 servings

Ingredients:

2 heads of garlic

3 tablespoons (50 ml) olive oil

5 tablespoons flour

1 teaspoon sweet paprika

Salt and pepper, to taste

3 double prime-cut veal
chops, 30 oz (800 g) each,
trimmed of all fat

6 tablespoons (100 g) butter

5 tablespoons dry white wine

1 tablespoon *pastis*

Several parsley stems

**Several hours in advance:** Peel the cloves from the garlic heads, removing any green germs from each clove center (they are hard to digest and cause "garlic breath"). Cut cloves lengthwise into strips. Heat the oil in a sauté pan. Add the garlic strips and cook gently over low heat until dry and lightly golden. Drain and set aside on paper toweling.

Combine the flour and paprika. Salt and pepper both sides of the veal chops. Dredge both sides in the flour-paprika mixture, pressing on the chops to help the flour adhere.

Over a moderate heat, using a combination stovetop-oven baking pan, heat 3 tablespoons (50 g) of the butter. When the butter begins to sizzle, place the veal chops flat in the pan. Cook until golden brown on both sides, about 10 minutes in all. Remove the veal chops from the pan and place them on a warm plate. Cover with foil so they continue to steam.

Pour the wine in the baking dish. Bring to a boil, then scrape the bottom with a wooden spatula to release the *sucs* (bits of caramelized meat and juices stuck on the bottom of the pan).

**25 minutes before serving:** Preheat oven to 400°F (200°C). Put remaining butter in the baking dish over low heat. Whisk it into the cooking juices, binding them lightly. Add the juices rendered from the chops. Add the *pastis*. Into a bowl, pour the sauce through a fine mesh strainer. Set aside in a warm area.

**5 minutes before serving:** Cut the veal chops in half and place them in the baking dish in the oven. Heat for 2–3 minutes, just until they are warmed through to the center. Place them on 6 hot plates. Nap with the sauce and sprinkle with the garlic strips. Scatter on several sprigs of fresh parsley. Serve immediately.

**Wine suggestion:** To hold up to the *pastis* while marrying with the finesse of the veal, I prefer a good regional wine with a robust flavor such as a red Coteaux Aix-en-Provence, *charpenté* (a robust wine from a good year) and a bit strong, which I serve at 57–61°F (14–16°C).

## Le soufflé léger aux reinettes
### (Light Reinette Apple Soufflé)

~

**Several hours in advance:** Peel and core 2 of the apples. Cut them into quarters. Put the 8 quarters in a saucepan with 2 tablespoons water and 2 tablespoons of the sugar. Cover and cook until the apples begin to break down. Whisk to further break down the apples into a compote. Take the pan off the heat and set aside to cool.

Peel and core the 2 remaining apples. Cut them into small cubes about ⅓-inch square (7–8 mm square). Heat 2 tablespoons (30 g) of the butter in a sauté pan. When the butter starts to foam, add the apple cubes and sauté for 3–4 minutes over high heat. Set aside to cool.

Butter 6 ramekins, 4 inches (10 cm) in diameter. Pour the granulated sugar into one of the ramekins and rotate it so the sugar adheres evenly to the bottom and sides. Pour the excess sugar into a second ramekin and rotate it to coat it evenly. Repeat this step until all the ramekins are coated with sugar. Set them on a baking pan so they do not touch and place them in the refrigerator.

Preparation: 25 minutes
Cooking: 30 minutes

Ease: Moderately difficult
Cost: Inexpensive
Yield: 6 servings

Ingredients:
4 reinette apples
(or Granny Smiths)
½ cup plus 2 tablespoons
superfine sugar
4 tablespoons (60 g) butter
12 eggs
6 tablespoons Calvados

**25 minutes before serving:** Preheat the oven to 400°F (210°C). Separate the eggs into two large bowls. Add 4 tablespoons sugar to the egg yolks, whisking them immediately for 5 minutes until they are pale and aerated. Stir in the apple compote and Calvados. Blend the mixture with a whisk. Gently fold in the cooked diced apple with a rubber spatula.

Beat the egg whites to firm peaks. Gently fold ⅓ of the whipped whites into the egg yolk base mixture. Incorporate the remaining whipped whites, folding from the bottom upward, making sure to scrape all the way down to the bottom of the bowl.

Fill the molds so they are slightly domed on top. Run your thumb around the rim of the mold so the edges of the mixture are even (don't hesitate to lick your thumb if nobody is looking).

Bake the soufflés for 3–4 minutes. Lower the temperature to 300°F (150°C). Cook for 10 minutes more without opening the oven.

Place the fully risen soufflés on dessert plates lined with doilies or folded napkins. Serve immediately.

**Chef's tip:** To perfectly whip the egg whites, refer to the "Chef's tip" on page 85.

*The modest apple is turned into a luxurious dish in this spectacular and economical recipe.*

# MENU INDEX

~

THE HERBS OF PROVENCE ............................................... 31
Orange Wine Punch ........................................................ 32
Artichoke and Wild Thyme Soup ................................... 33
Mussels and Fennel with Saffron Cream Sauce .............. 35
Lavender Ice Cream with Small Anise Cookies .............. 39

A LUNCHEON UNDER THE ARBOR ................................. 43
Vergé's Orange Cocktail ................................................ 44
Warm Rock-Lobster Salad with Orange Butter Sauce ...... 45
Lamb and Eggplant Timbales ........................................ 47
Niçoise Vegetable Compote ........................................... 50
Crêpes in Honey with Provençal Pine Nuts ................... 51

TUTTI FRUTTI ............................................................... 55
Fruit and Wine Cocktail ................................................ 55
Chilled Melon Soup with Wild Strawberries .................. 57
Chicken Fricassee with Fresh Figs in Port Sauce ........... 58
Assorted Fruit and Almond Cream Terrine .................... 61

IN THE HOLIDAY SPIRIT ................................................ 65
Fresh Tuna and Salmon Gazpacho ................................ 66
Crayfish Salad with Cream Sauce .................................. 67
Red Fruit Cocktail with Champagne ............................. 72

A LUNCHEON OF FLOWERS ............................................ 75
Champagne with Orange ............................................... 76
Stuffed Zucchini Flowers with Truffles ......................... 77
Roast Rack of Lamb with Thyme Flowers ...................... 80
Orange Meringue Tartlets with Lavender Flowers ......... 82
Poppy Liqueur ............................................................. 85

A PARTY MENU ............................................................. 87
Scrambled Eggs in their Shells with Caviar ................... 89
Lobster Fricassee with Tarragon Cream Sauce .............. 91
Lamb Fillets in Puff Pastry with Duxelle of Wild Mushrooms ... 92
Frozen Strawberry Soufflés ........................................... 97

# Menu Index

~

DINNER AT THE MOUGINS .......................................................... 101
Mougins-Style Olive Tart ........................................................... 103
Chicken Legs with Aromatic Vegetables and Lemon ............... 104
Seasonal Fruit Tartlets ................................................................ 107

AUNT CÉLESTINE'S DINNER ..................................................... 109
Peach-Flavored Champagne ....................................................... 109
Terrines of Tarragon-Flavored Sea Bass ................................... 110
Casserole of Pigeon with Small Peas ........................................ 112
Light Apricot Charlotte .............................................................. 115

A SPRING FEAST ......................................................................... 119
Mouginoise Salad ....................................................................... 121
Spring Lamb Stew with Baby Vegetables .................................. 123
Apricot and Almond Gratins with Kirsch Syrup ..................... 127

SCENTS AND SPICES .................................................................. 129
Roasted Sweet Red Pepper and Anchovy Compote ................. 130
Roasted Royal Sea Bream with Savory and Ginger-Orange Butter ...... 131
Peaches or Pears Poached in Pepper and Bay-Leaf Scented Wine ...... 134

A MENU FOR CLOSE FRIENDS ................................................. 137
Cardinal ...................................................................................... 138
Sweet Garlic Soup ...................................................................... 139
Shell Steak with Anchovies and Herbs ...................................... 140
Individual Apple Walnut Tarts .................................................. 141

AN AUTUMN LUNCHEON .......................................................... 143
White Wine with Walnut Liqueur ............................................. 143
Creamy Morel Quiche ................................................................ 145
Veal Chops with Anise and Garlic ............................................. 148
Light Reinette Apple Soufflé ..................................................... 149

# RECIPE INDEX

~

Apricot and Almond Gratins with Kirsch Syrup .......................................... 127

Artichoke and Wild Thyme Soup .......................................... 33

Assorted Fruit and Almond Cream Terrine .......................................... 61

Cardinal .......................................... 138

Casserole of Pigeon with Small Peas .......................................... 112

Champagne with Orange .......................................... 76

Chicken Fricassee with Fresh Figs in Port Sauce .......................................... 58

Chicken Legs with Aromatic Vegetables and Lemon .......................................... 104

Chilled Melon Soup with Wild Strawberries .......................................... 57

Crayfish Salad with Cream Sauce .......................................... 67

Creamy Morel Quiche .......................................... 145

Crêpes in Honey with Provençal Pine Nuts .......................................... 51

Fresh Tuna and Salmon Gazpacho .......................................... 66

Frozen Strawberry Soufflés .......................................... 97

Fruit and Wine Cocktail .......................................... 55

Herbed Fromage Blanc .......................................... 120

Individual Apple Walnut Tarts .......................................... 141

Lamb and Eggplant Timbales .......................................... 47

Lamb Fillets in Puff Pastry with Duxelle of Wild Mushrooms .......................................... 92

Lavender Ice Cream with Small Anise Cookies .......................................... 39

Light Apricot Charlotte .......................................... 115

Light Reinette Apple Soufflé .......................................... 149

Lobster Fricassee with Tarragon Cream Sauce .......................................... 91

Mougins-Style Olive Tart .......................................... 103

# RECIPE INDEX

~

Mouginoise Salad ............................................................................ 121
Mussels and Fennel with Saffron Cream Sauce .............................. 35
Niçoise Vegetable Compote .............................................................. 50
Orange Meringue Tartlets with Lavender Flowers ........................... 82
Orange Wine Punch ........................................................................... 32
Peaches or Pears Poached in Pepper and Bay-Leaf Scented Wine ..... 134
Poppy Liqueur .................................................................................... 85
Red Fruit Cocktail with Champagne ................................................. 72
Roast Rack of Lamb with Thyme Flowers ........................................ 80
Roasted Royal Sea Bream with Savory and Ginger-Orange Butter .... 131
Roasted Sweet Red Pepper and Anchovy Compote ......................... 130
Scrambled Eggs in their Shells with Caviar ..................................... 89
Seasonal Fruit Tartlets ...................................................................... 107
Shell Steak with Anchovies and Herbs ............................................ 140
Spring Lamb Stew with Baby Vegetables ......................................... 123
Stuffed Zucchini Flowers with Truffles ............................................ 77
Sweet Garlic Soup ............................................................................. 139
Terrines of Tarragon-Flavored Sea Bass .......................................... 110
Veal Chops with Anise and Garlic .................................................... 148
Vergé's Orange Cocktail .................................................................... 44
Warm Rock-Lobster Salad with Orange Butter Sauce ..................... 45
White Wine with Walnut Liqueur .................................................... 143

# A la Carte

~

APÉRITIFS AND DRINKS
Cardinal ........................................................................ 138
Champagne with Orange ............................................ 76
Peach-Flavored Champagne ....................................... 109
Vergé's Orange Cocktail ............................................ 44
Fruit and Wine Cocktail ............................................ 55
Poppy Liqueur ........................................................... 85
Vermouth-cassis ........................................................ 138
White Wine with Walnut Liqueur .............................. 143
Orange Wine Punch ................................................... 32

APPETIZERS
Herbed Fromage Blanc .............................................. 120
Toasts with Sautéed Porcini ...................................... 144
Toasts with truffle ..................................................... 88

SOUPS
Fresh Tuna and Salmon Gazpacho ............................. 66
Artichoke and Wild Thyme Soup ............................... 33
Sweet Garlic Soup ..................................................... 139

ENTRÉES
Roasted Sweet Red Pepper and Anchovy Compote ..... 130
Stuffed Zucchini Flowers with Truffles ..................... 77
Chilled Melon Soup with Wild Strawberries .............. 57
Creamy Morel Quiche ................................................ 145
Mougins-Style Olive Tart .......................................... 103

# A la Carte

~

EGGS
Scrambled Eggs in their Shells with Caviar ........................................ 89
Mouginoise Salad ................................................................................ 121

SEAFOOD
Lobster Fricassee with Tarragon Cream Sauce .................................. 91
Mussels and Fennel in Saffron Cream Sauce .................................... 35
Crayfish Salad with Cream Sauce ...................................................... 67
Warm Rock-Lobster Salad with Orange Butter Sauce ...................... 45
Terrines of Tarragon-Flavored Sea Bass ............................................ 110
Roasted Royal Sea Bream with Savory and Ginger-Orange Butter ........ 131

POULTRY
Chicken Legs with Aromatic Vegetables and Lemon ........................ 104
Chicken Fricassee with Fresh Figs in Port Sauce ............................ 58
Casserole of Pigeon with Small Peas ................................................ 112

MEAT
Roast Rack of Lamb with Thyme Flowers ........................................ 80
Veal Chops with Anise and Garlic .................................................... 148
Shell Steak with Anchovies and Herbs ............................................ 140
Lamb Fillets in Puff Pastry with Duxelle of Wild Mushrooms ........ 92
Lamb and Eggplant Timbales ............................................................ 47
Spring Lamb Stew with Baby Vegetables .......................................... 123

*(Continued on next page)*

# A la Carte

~

VEGETABLES
Niçoise Vegetable Compote ........................................................ 50

DESSERTS
Light Apricot Charlotte ............................................................ 115
Red Fruit Cocktail with Champagne ........................................ 72
Crêpes in Honey with Provençal Pine Nuts .............................. 51
Lavender Ice Cream with Small Anise Cookies ......................... 39
Apricot and Almond Gratins with Kirsch Syrup .................... 127
Frozen Strawberry Soufflés ...................................................... 97
Soufflé léger aux reinettes ...................................................... 149
Individual Apple Walnut Tarts .............................................. 141
Seasonal Fruit Tartlets ........................................................... 107
Orange Meringue Tartlets with Lavender Flowers .................. 82
Assorted Fruit and Almond Cream Terrine .............................. 61
Peaches or Pears Poached in Pepper and Bay-Leaf Scented Wine ...... 134

COFFEES
Café "Bistouille" ..................................................................... 28
Café Brûlot ............................................................................. 28
Irish Coffee ............................................................................ 28
Café Royal .............................................................................. 28

# ACKNOWLEDGMENTS

~

This book would never have seen the light of day without the work of the team that helped bring all the ingredients together. I would like to thank all those who shared in this collaboration.

First, my gratitude goes to Charles-Henri Flammarion, who accepted this ambitious project and gave me the possibility to work with photographer Pierre Hussenot. I have appreciated Monsieur Hussenot's calm and discretion over the course of the long weeks of shooting.

I would like to send my gratitude to my editor, Gisou Bavoillot, and her staff, who supported me step by step throughout the realization of this work.

I would like to next thank all those who contributed to the recipe testing: Jean-Jacques Trilhe, Serge Chollet, and Denis Mornet. Thanks to Danièle Schnapp, who helped us at the beginning of the photography shoots.

This book is meant for entertaining at home. Therefore, none of the photos were taken at the Moulin de Mougins. Some were taken at my home, others at the homes of friends who warmly welcomed our rather invading crew. I would also like to give recognition to Line and Roger Mühl, César, Bernard Chevry, Madame Costa, Mesdames Polverino, and Monsieur Chemit. Some of these names can be found again in acknowledgments reserved for those good friends who had the difficult task of partaking in the luncheon under the linden tree. Seated at the table were: César, Roger Mühl, Bernard Chevry, José Albertini, and Patrick d'Humières.

Thanks also to all those who furnished us with ingredients and props for the recipes: Robert and Édouard Céneri, who make the great cheeses at La Ferme Savoyarde, and Georges Bruger, La Roi du Charolais; and to the following boutiques: Au Bain Marie (20 rue Hérold, 75001 Paris), Ateliers de Segriès (Moustiers Ste-Marie), Dîners en Ville (27 rue de Varenne, 75007 Paris), Christian Dior (30 Avenue Montaigne, 75008 Paris), Pierre Frey (47 rue des Petits-Champs, 75002 Paris), Primrose Bordier (57 Avenue d'Iéna, 75016 Paris), Descamps (88 rue de Rivoli, 75004 Paris), La Tuile à Loup (35 rue Daubenton, 75005 Paris), Geneviève Lethu (95 rue de Rennes, 75005 Paris), Pier Import (122 rue de Rivoli, 75004 Paris), Au Pérou (Cannes), Soleïado (1 rue Lobineau, 75006 Paris), Verreries de Biot (Biot).

I would like to especially thank Serge Cholet, Michel Duhamel, and Daniel Desavie, without forgetting Sylvie Charbit, who brought their care and talent to this book.

The editor would very much like to express his deepest gratitude to Andy Stewart, who presided over the birth of the first edition of *Roger Vergé's Entertaining in the French Style* from which this new work was born, and to Adeline Brousse, Marc Walter, Margherita Mariano, Muriel Vaux, and Anne-Laure Mojaïsky for their collaboration on this new edition.

Printed in Italy by G. Canale & C. S.p.A. - Borgaro T.se - TURIN

...rabe tiède

d'Épices et de fruits.

...légumes en gelée de

vinaigre d'épices aux feuilles

d'Estragon et de Basilic.

marmi... ~~ojoux~~ grandes Montm...

...les en Crème de Roquefort.

...du Var en Bâtonnets —

...de l'Ailloli en tapenade

...des petits légumes et

...de Cerfeuil.

Rognon de Veau Santos

...Madère

500
g
a